"I stand in awe and admi
and the Churches represent and do. All businesses
should aspire to be like them...and the world
would be a better place because of it!"

— JIMBO SOMECK
Founder, Jimbo's Naturally

"A hands on, practical guide to help you create
enduring family memories while strengthening
your community and changing the world. Jeff
and Linda illustrate the lasting legacy they are
creating with their children as they work to
bring clean water and hope to all parts of the
world."

— SUSIE NORDENGER
Community Service Director,
La Jolla Country Day School

A THIRST for CHANGE

A THIRST *for* CHANGE

How Social Entrepreneurship Can Make the World a Better Place

Linda & Jeff Church

Church Family Productions
San Diego, CA

Church Family Productions
Jeff Church
PO Box 2348
La Jolla, CA 92038
Phone: 1-800-545-5841
Fax: 928-441-7589

First Edition

ISBN: 978-0-9836406-0-8 (Case Bound Book)
ISBN: 978-0-9836406-2-2 (Paperback)
ISBN: 978-0-9836406-3-9 (eBook)

Library of Congress Control Number: 2011929556

Text Design by Dotti Albertine

Dedication

To our beautiful mothers, Judy and Rachel,
who taught us at the earliest of ages
the importance of giving to one's capacity.

To Nina, Joshua, Rachel and Jacob,
may you live a life not only of success
but more importantly a life of significance.

To our wonderful brothers, sisters, nieces and nephews
who have shared and helped so much with this incredible journey.

To the Stone family, Mike, Karen, Rachel, Sammy and Wyatt.
Your desire and support to launch Nika and forever
transform lives has been a powerful motivator for all of us.

Contents

Acknowledgments

WE WOULD LIKE TO thank Michael Levin and his team for making this book happen so quickly and easily.

We would also like to thank our dear friend, Ken Druck, who gave us the confidence and inspired us to move forward with this incredible project.

Our love, appreciation and admiration also go out to Stephen Bennett for the donation of his incredible artwork to the labels for our bottles. Stephen's dedication to support the impoverished around the world is felt deeply in our hearts. Through his beautiful portraits he provides vibrancy and hope to so many.

Introduction

WE WRITE THIS in the aftermath of the Japanese tsunami. The horrific images of waves rushing over people, buildings and towns leave an indelible imprint. But alongside such images are those equally indelible which show humanity at its finest. The heroic rescue efforts to deliver the displaced and dispossessed to higher ground provide an apt metaphor for what our book is about. Japan's tragedy reminds us that disasters happen with depressing frequency. Indeed, there is no shortage of problems to tackle. From health issues to malnutrition to human and animal rights to poverty, the list goes on and on. But so too does the search for a solution to each and every one of these problems. And it is in this search that we discover our higher ground—a place where we ennoble ourselves in the service of others.

This is the story of a company that sells water in America to help those around the world trapped in poverty. We hope our story inspires you. We also hope it provides you with a tool—a tool to build a business dedicated to serving a cause of your own choosing. We hope that you will find in the story of NIKA not just the story of a company that tries to make the world a better place, but a template for each and every one of us to follow our passions and make a difference.

The world has changed. For the business-minded, it used to be that you'd get a job in a corporation, toe the line, work your way up, wait years and years, and then finally seek a chance to make a difference. The old business model was to make a profit. Now, don't get us wrong. We're all for the profit motive. We believe deeply in the power of the free market to create jobs, opportunity, and all manner of goods and services. It's just that today, with information bombarding us by the minute, people are less likely to say, "I'm going to work to make money, and the rest of the world must care for itself." A new business model has emerged to challenge this notion. It says that creating personal wealth and helping others are not mutually exclusive. This new business model allows people to do both and it is nothing short of a fundamental paradigm shift. It's called "social entrepreneurship."

Social entrepreneurship means starting, or working for, a business that seeks to solve a public problem instead of generating profit as its primary objective. For instance, Newman's Own has donated more than $300 million over the past twenty-five years to numerous causes and charities just through the sale of salad dressing and soups! The NIKA business is similar. Our business turns a profit *solely* for the purpose of combating a social ill: 100% of the profits from NIKA help bring clean water and education to people around the globe. So today you can have something unimagined only a short time ago: a business career that tackles society's ills.

How about you? What's your passion?

What challenge would you like to help solve?

Whatever it is, you can start now. You don't have to wait to make a difference, in the corporate world or in life. This is another fundamental paradigm shift. Individuals now create entire companies from a dorm room with their laptop. Think about all the tech companies—from Microsoft and Apple to Google and Facebook—that were created without huge overhead or investment. The opportunity to catalyze positive change in the world is indeed a click away.

You too can create a company, or find one to work for, that makes money...and makes a difference.

That's what our book is about.

Actually, that's what *your* book is about. We say this because we want you to be *extremely* successful in your business career so you can help make a difference in someone's life.

However, the first part of this book is our story—who we are as well as how and why we were inspired to create NIKA.

The second part is about the concept of social entrepreneurship, so you can learn about this exciting innovation and how it can help solve tough global challenges.

The third part is all about you—how you can create or join an enterprise dedicated to social entrepreneurship.

We've presented our story to hopefully inspire you and provide you with tools to either continue your journey if you've already started it or to be a catalyst to help you start thinking about your passion and your ideas. We described social entrepreneurship so that you can understand the movement. Finally, we've set forth how to get involved and develop such a business so that you may discover your higher ground and deliver those in need to it. That's why we say this is a book about you. It's not just about what we're seeking to accomplish. It's about how you can contribute to the world, and maximize the enjoyment, meaning, and success you create for yourself and for the rest of us.

Sincerely,
Linda and Jeff Church

Part One

The NIKA Story

*Nothing is softer
or more flexible than water,
yet nothing can resist it.*

– Lao Tzu –

CHAPTER 1

Getting Our Feet Wet

Destiny is not a matter of chance. It's a matter of choice.
It's not a thing to be waited for. It's a thing to be achieved.
– William Jennings Bryan –

Can a bottle of water save the world?

What if a bottled water company committed to donating its profits to dig wells for communities in the poorest parts of the planet?

And what if that business model—sell, and devote profits to solving a major world problem—were to be borrowed by other individuals creating their own companies, selling their own products and solving other problems?

Maybe a bottle of water *could help* save the world.

Here's the problem. Charitable organizations often lack steady sources of funding. They can have a vital mission but lack the ongoing income necessary to keep their dream alive. Or they can have leaders with an amazing vision of transforming the world…but lacking in the business know-how to turn their vision into reality.

What if social entrepreneurship stepped in to fill this gap? Entrepreneurs are business people who know how to make dreams come true, for themselves, their investors, their employees, and their customers. Social entrepreneurship means creating a business that does more than spin off money. It also creates change.

Here's the next problem: many people, especially young people, who have a desire to create sustainable change in the world, think business is all about greed and exploitation. It can be, of course. But there's nothing inherently evil about the business world. So the people who *could be* social entrepreneurs first have to learn that business is a tool for creating anything. Not just profits, but change.

Business can make people's lives better, not just here but anywhere in the world.

This book is the story of a little company with a big idea: sell bottled water. Use the profits to dig wells in desperately poor regions. Eliminate the struggle to bring clean water to the village, a struggle that consumes the lives of women and girls and frequently means that education ends when the need to bring water begins. Transform communities. Save lives.

And then inspire others to use this model of social entrepreneurship and create businesses of their own, founded on the idea of devoting profits to solving problems. More businesses started equates to more jobs here and more problems solved elsewhere on the planet.

We're Linda and Jeff Church. We were fortunate enough to achieve a respectable level of success in the business world. We had reached the point in our lives when we wanted to move beyond financial success to life significance, to making a difference, and to demonstrating to our children the importance of not just giving back but creating something that can have the potential to leave a lasting impact on the world.

We're doing it with water.

You can do it with anything, and you can solve any problem in the world. Anyone can be a social entrepreneur. This book will show you how.

So who are we? Who are your guides on what we hope will be your path to social entrepreneurship?

Like most dynamic partnerships, we brought distinctly different experiences and skills to our relationship. At the same time, as we began to know each other, we realized that, despite the difference in our backgrounds, we possessed remarkably similar values and goals on both the personal and global level.

Linda's story begins in Casablanca, Morocco, where she was born and spent the first few years of her life. Her mother was a courageous woman, willing to face great hardship for the sake of giving her four children a better future. With virtually no assets or support, Rachel Hazan immigrated with her four children to North America, living in Montreal for four years while waiting for a United States green card. As in many marriages arranged in the old country, Linda's parents were not happy together. Despite the hand that life had dealt her, Linda's mom never wavered in her commitment to the continuity of the core identity of her family.

The early years in America were a time when life was not at all easy. The family was very poor, and Linda grew up sharing one room with her three siblings. Even at a young age, it was essential that she also work to support the household, be it cleaning homes, doing dishes, sewing or baking with her mother. Nonetheless, Linda's mother impressed on the children that their future would be better here in the United States. She taught them that with this country's amazing opportunities for self-improvement also came responsibilities. As they went through life, she said, they would each have to work and earn everything they received.

In addition to the American work ethic that she so readily adopted, Linda's mom brought with her from Morocco a strong identification with both the philosophy and the culture of her family's Jewish heritage. She raised the children with the words of the Torah as their guide, calling it "life's instructions" to each generation. One of the most important values she gave her children was the value of "JNF tzedakah box," which means "justice and charity." Linda's mother taught them at a very young age to be grateful and gracious with whatever they had. There were always people in worse shape than they were, so it was always necessary to give back. Every day, each family member had to put a few pennies in the special "JNK tzedakah box" kept at home to collect this generosity.

Even amid the sacred commitment to hard work, heritage and charity, Linda's mom's marital misery became unbearable. Like many immigrant couples, the new surroundings only intensified the problems felt back home. But Linda's mom quickly learned that in America, women do not have to remain in abusive relationships. With the help of Jewish Family Services, she got an attorney and achieved her independence. For a brief time, she even needed to accept food stamps. She was so proud, however, that she would only go to the market in the middle of the night so no one would see her taking handouts.

Jeff's own childhood was about as opposite from that as you could possibly imagine. Growing up in Cleveland, Ohio, his father was a Chief Financial Officer of a local company while his mother was a teacher. Jeff enjoyed the comfort and stability of this typical American middle class environment, performing so highly in his newspaper delivery route that at age thirteen he won a trip to Florida until then only given to sixteen-year-olds. Just a few years later, he was taking on "real" jobs such as janitorial work, sweeping amphitheaters and shopping centers in Chautauqua Lake, New York.

Jeff's mother provided an excellent example of the family's continuing commitment to make a positive difference in as many lives as possible. She was a giving person possessing not just intelligence but what's called "emotional intelligence." Jeff's mother had been a teacher throughout her career, committed to early childhood education long before it became a major topic of discussion in our society. Early on, she was teaching kids during daycare before people were calling it daycare. Later, she started the first inter-generational daycare center. Recognizing that there were elders who didn't have much to do and were looking for companionship, she matched them with children who needed early education and daycare. This was incredibly useful to the community, because the adult/child ratios at that grade level were very low. Since the number of children per adult was so limited, each elder person became very valuable to the program. Without realizing she was doing it, she created a new and effective new teaching— and business—model. Soon after, this program won a bunch of awards.

—Jeff talks about growing up—

I went to public schools and enjoyed the experience—particularly sports. In hindsight, I was fortunate that our school's teams were not very good—and I will explain why. Our football team always lost, but one memorable afternoon we got very close to winning. I was playing wide receiver, and I actually caught a few good passes including one for a touchdown. Late in the game, we were only down by a few points. Clearly, this was going to be the best personal performance of my mediocre two-year career.

With victory almost in grasp, I made a personal mistake that haunted me for many years after. I was running a pattern in the end zone, and the quarterback rolling out didn't see that I was open. That very split second, I made a decision not to raise my hand as available to catch the pass. You would have thought that I would have wanted more than anything to catch a second touchdown pass. I did, but greater than my anticipation of success was my fear of dropping this easy pass and thus wiping away my accomplishments up until then. Naturally, since I wasn't calling for the ball, the quarterback didn't see me, didn't throw to me—and was tackled behind the line. Thanks to my timidity and my placing "perfection" over achievement—we lost again.

For many years, I was upset about my decision in that end zone. But as I matured and gained life experiences, that painful event actually became a learning opportunity, teaching me that you *do* have to raise your hand in life to get ahead. I came to recognize that it's really important in life to push yourself out of your comfort zone; if you don't raise your hand (even if you're a little intimidated) no one is going to throw you the ball. As I became an adult, I grew much more concerned about wallowing in mediocrity than about occasionally facing failure.

After high school, I went to Michigan State University, and I remain a proud Spartan to this day. I studied accounting, and was involved with many school activities. It was the smoothest introduction anyone could have to the "real world."

For my first job after college, I was fortunate to get hired by Ernst &

Young for a job in public accounting. I got my CPA, and recognized that accounting was the language of business. This background provided me with a great foundation for business. But as the months and years went by, I became progressively convinced that I didn't want to be an accountant all my life. Then, I was fortunate to get assigned to the Merger and Acquisition group within Ernst and Young. Three years out of college, with a lot of different business experiences under my belt, I was accepted into the MBA program at Harvard Business School.

After those two years of graduate work, I had planned to head off to Wall Street. But an opportunity arose to spend a few months with my good friend and HBS classmate, Steve Heese, working on a troubled company in New Jersey. Even though we both had Wall Street jobs already lined up, we knew that this challenge was much closer to the direction we wanted to be heading: to run, and then hopefully become owners, of companies we had either restored or built from scratch. The excitement and better pay of Wall Street would have to take second place to our serious long-term goals. So my buddy and I jumped into this assignment, our first real job as consultants.

After thoroughly reviewing all aspects of the company, we presented our consulting report to the owner of the company. It was the standard twenty page "outside expert" document, where we listed everything that was wrong with the company and projected what would happen if management did not address these issues. The owner's response was swift and direct: *"Well, if you really believe that, why don't you two stay and fix it?"*

That's when I learned that, in life as in a lot of other activities, implementation is a lot more difficult than consultation. Working off our twenty-page report, Steve and I figured that we could get the job done in about three months. As it turned out, we spent a good two years on the project.

For all the wisdom I absorbed in this assignment, and for all the success we created, there was a far larger benefit to my relocating to New Jersey: that's how I met Linda. This relationship would soon become a joining of two wildly different cultures and styles. We both had business backgrounds, but we were coming from different directions. Linda was very entrepreneurial, and I was more of the traditional managerial type. But together, it became an excellent marriage not just of people but of business skills!

Since we met in a business environment, that's where our story goes next. This was 1989, just at the beginning of the era of personal information devices where cell phones were just becoming portable, and they were large! Linda and her brother owned the local retail cellular phone store near where I worked.

—Linda recalls how they got to that point—

My brother David had started the original business out of my mom's garage with a very good idea. Working part time at a video store at a time when cable television was becoming more widespread, he noticed that many people were returning their VCR purchases even though nothing was mechanically wrong with the machine. Quickly, he realized that the problem was that people couldn't figure out how to hook up the VCR to work with their cable service.

My brother had identified a new consumer need—and a new business. On our neighbor's relatively primitive Apple computer, we created a simple brochure for this new service called VCI—Video and Cable Installation. Our message was "Don't get shook up, get hooked up."

Next came the marketing. I literally took those little pamphlets to every department store and every store that sold VCRs. My sales pitch was simple: "How many VCRs are you getting back? Don't take these VCRs back, there's nothing wrong with them. We'll send somebody out to install it for a fixed fee of $35."

My brother trained a couple of his friends to handle the service calls. They'd go into people's homes, hook up their VCRs, and then give a quick little instruction on how to use the machine with the cable service. We ended up doing really well, developing some really excellent customers who loved our customer service and the way we took care of them. This was where we learned the importance and benefits of treating your customers honestly, kindly and fairly.

It was from this satisfied customer base that we got our next great opportunity. They were the ones who recommended us to a new cellular network that would be offering service in our area. The company came down and interviewed us, and we got the contract.

So, we ended up in a full-fledged entrepreneurial business without a really strong educational or management background. I had gone to high school and then straight to work. We made a lot of errors and learned a lot along the way. We were always really risk takers, trying new things and seeing where the market would take us. Thanks to our hard work and some good timing, our company did well.

—Jeff continues the story at the phone store—

When I arrived at the store to get a car phone, it was Linda who offered to show me some of the new models. By the time she came back with the first phone for me to inspect, that was pretty much the end of it; I wanted to connect further with this attractive, intelligent woman.

I didn't waste much time. After my purchase, they quickly installed the phone in my car and it was time to leave. On my way out, Linda suggested I call someone to test the phone. Naturally, I chose to call her. I told her that I was fairly new in town and asked if she would go out on a date. Soon, we had a pretty serious relationship.

For me, it was exposure to a culture about which I knew very little. I had no idea what a Moroccan Jew was, let alone that there was even such a thing as a Moroccan Jew, because I grew up in a very insulated, meat and potatoes environment. To me, Linda and her family were exotic!

Linda says that when Jeff came into her life it was really just fun. She was preoccupied with running three companies plus dealing with family matters.

At first she thought that the friendship would never become more than just a fun distraction for her at this time in her life. But gradually, she realized that for the first time she had someone who cared for her not because of her "role" as sister, business partner, or daughter. Instead, Jeff was interested in her for who she was. As they got to know each other, and Linda got to know his family, especially his mom, she found Jeff to be a really authentic, generous, kind human being. She says that within the first year, they both knew. She fell in love with him because of the values that they shared and the vision of the kind of life they wanted to build together.

Linda quickly found acceptance from Jeff's family. If you can envision the movie, *My Big Fat Greek Wedding*, that's pretty much the scene. Just swap Greek for Moroccan. The first time Linda met his mom, she confided that she was excited Linda was Jewish because if they got married, "I won't have to share him at Christmas!" In fact, she was even more excited about Linda's faith in God, which compared favorably in her eyes to her own son's generally agnostic views at the time.

Jeff's mom came through at a critical point in our relationship. After being pretty serious, we then had reversed course and decided that maybe we shouldn't get married and maybe we shouldn't spend our lives together. Jeff was then 27, and in no particular rush to get married. Worried about losing Linda, his mom called her and asked her to give her son one more chance. Linda did, and they soon were engaged and then married three months later.

Linda knew how important it was to her mom that her daughter not marry outside of her faith. Linda prayed a lot and eventually came to peace with what she was doing. It was a difficult challenge for Linda to say, "You know, I know this is the right thing."

We made a point of dealing with these personal religious issues before we got married. Jeff understood how important Linda's Judaism was to her and how important it was to her to raise her children as Jews. We came to an understanding that we would raise our kids with a Jewish education, but the actual location of our home would have to be flexible enough to shift to wherever Jeff's career took him. Linda likes to tell people that she's probably the only person with a last name "Church" that keeps a kosher home!

While our backgrounds may have been different, as a married unit we soon realized that we were very similar—maybe too much so. Usually in a relationship, one spouse is the "giver" and the other, guarding the checkbook, is more restrained. In our case we're both "givers": there's virtually no fiscal restraint. Whenever we have identified a cause that is close to us or our family members, we tend to give almost without limit. We're proud of that, but of course without some limits we wouldn't be able to continue doing what we do.

—Jeff picks up the story—

Late one night, I was up channel surfing. On the TV was a bunch of senior citizens being interviewed and for some reason, I stopped and watched as the interviewer went around the room asking each of them, looking back, what they wished they had done differently in their lives. I was startled to hear that every single one of them said that they wished they had taken more risk in their professional careers.

It was hearing the testimony of these candid senior citizens that gave me the clarity to know that I was at a natural point to leave my prior employer and go off on my own. I worked out a really nice exit arrangement with the company that was followed by spending three months taking care of things and helping them find a replacement. I explained to my disappointed friends at work that this was the time in my life that I needed to go out and buy a company.

Finding the right company involved both personal and professional considerations. Since my background was manufacturing, that was the focus of our search. We drew a circle around the Midwest because that's where most of my contacts were. Linda wanted to be close to her family, who had mostly migrated to Southern California. Her dream was to be close enough to family so that they could all spend the Jewish holidays together, as they did when they were young. When things got serious with a Midwestern acquisition, Linda, her mother and her sisters literally prayed that something else would work out. In the end, their prayers were answered: we ended up finding a company in Los Angeles. I had missed my "target" by about 2,500 miles, but things were looking upbeat. Things went well in the new venture, and the risk we took was amply rewarded.

So there we were, approaching our fortieth birthdays, with the question of "Now what?" firmly imprinted on our minds as well as a deep concern that we would raise "spoiled" children given the environment that they would be raised in. We've always challenged ourselves to make sure that our children felt a responsibility to humanity versus an entitlement to stuff. This has always been a stress point to make sure that we find teachable ways to have our children internalize these beliefs. Our desires and our pasts laid the foundations for our family trip to Africa, which would eventually inspire the story you are about to read.

We never imagined where the road would take us next: to water and a chance to use our business skills to do our small part in making the world a better place. How we made the decision to start NIKA is the subject of the next chapter.

CHAPTER 2

Diving In

*A hundred years from now it will not matter what my bank account
was, the sort of house I lived in, or the kind of car that I drove...but the
world may be different because I was important in the life of a child.*
—Anonymous –

*S*o HOW DO A couple of serial entrepreneurs suddenly get the idea to, in
their own way, make a difference in the world?

Everything has to do with the people with whom you surround yourself. When you're around inspiring people, you get inspired ideas. It's that
simple.

After our move to San Diego, our children's new school made a big
difference in their lives, and in ours. La Jolla Country Day had an amazing
community service program. We immediately connected with the director,
Susie Nordenger, who's an amazing human being herself. She embodies the
same philosophy we have about making community service a natural part
of your everyday life. At Country Day, she works with kids of all ages—
from three-year-olds to high school seniors—and her motto for all of them
is, "Service is a way of life."

Susie says that service "is a habit no different than brushing your teeth"
and teaches the kids to give a hand up versus a handout whenever possible.
Whether it's walking the young ones across the street to say thank you to
the firefighters or leading a service trip to Nicaragua, Susie pours her heart
into these kids.

Susie says, "I have an optimistic outlook because I know that if we're going to make a big change in the world, it's going to come through this generation."

Thanks to Susie's training, when a disaster hits a different part of the world, such as Hurricane Katrina or the tsunamis in Southeast Asia, the Country Day community's response is never, "Are we going to do something," but instead, "*What* are we going to do?" Susie inspires the kids to research the disaster and research possible relief options. "The kids are serious, they love it, they do their research, and then they come together once the decision's made and rally behind it," says Susie.

We loved Country Day as soon as we visited, and Susie's confidence in her students was a big selling point. She has said, "If I get an email someday that one of our kids—in his or her research—has hit that last niche in the cure for cancer or the fight against AIDS, I'm not going to be surprised. And someday, if one of our kids is a Nobel Prize winner or a politician, I'm not going to be surprised." Needless to say, we were thrilled when the school accepted the applications of all four of our kids.

From the first moment our kids enrolled in Country Day, they have been involved in both our projects and their own, either through their school life or through our family activities. Susie does a fantastic job training the kids to be service-minded and globally conscious in the same way that we've tried to teach them since they were young.

Giving starts at home—and our family grew increasingly active in our close San Diego community. As they got older, our kids inherited our spirit and showed a strong desire to contribute in a bigger way than just themselves. For example, when Nina was in sixth grade, she began tutoring the kids of Sudanese refugees. Nina says, "I tutored kids on my free time twice a week. I tutored a kindergartener from Sudan and really loved it. I got to know the refugee networks. It was always so amazing to me to hear their stories." It's no surprise that Nina eventually wanted to do a service project in Africa before we had even thought of it ourselves!

Our kids would even create their own mini-foundations. When they were younger, our daughter created something called *The Giving Heart*. In addition, our family banded together in several ways to serve the greater San Diego Jewish Community, which we still do now. Eventually, our eyes opened to even larger philanthropic needs that we might be able to address.

—Jeff says—

In between the different companies I bought and sold, I typically had some downtime to be able to focus on some other stuff. Linda and I have always been percolating what we refer to as "dream maker" ideas. We'd always had the idea to create a business that would nurture, support and finance different people's dreams. We envisioned bringing our business knowledge and helping people incubate, start and fulfill their dreams and aspirations. We had also been talking for some time about wanting to transition our lives from moderate business success to life significance. NIKA would eventually become the factor that would connect all those dots, which were just dreams and ideas for some time.

As it happens, one of my business partners/good friend and a former classmate of mine from business school, Mike Stone and his lovely wife, Karen, were also doing some similar soul searching. Mike had already created some wealth for himself and his family through his career, and he was looking for something similar in the area of service. Mike and I discussed how we might be able to join forces and make a difference together. We began to do some serious research, always trying to pinpoint exactly where we had both the potential and the capital to make a difference. We wanted to search the entire world, including the developed world, for ways to maximize our investment dollars and impact as many lives as possible. I scoured the Internet with the same tenacity I have when I perform due diligence in a business deal. And at this point, water—bottled or otherwise—was not on our minds.

We started to learn in depth about real poverty, where people are living on less than a dollar a day, with none of the basics we take for granted, such as clean water. Working through our research, we began to realize, "Boy, it doesn't take much money to make a difference!" In the developing world, your dollar goes a heck of a lot further than it does here.

One huge benefit of our research was the number of remarkable people we met along the way. These are people who we would have never encountered in our normal business and social circles. Some of them became instrumental in bringing our anti-poverty efforts to reality—and have also become lifelong friends.

In our research, we kept on bumping into references to an individual named Jeffrey Sachs. An economist and director of the Earth Institute at Columbia University, he led a group of people who initially created the Millennium Development Goals for the United Nations. These are a set of eight international development goals that all 192 United Nations member states and 23 international organizations have agreed to achieve by the year 2015. They include eradicating extreme poverty, reducing child mortality rates, fighting disease epidemics such as AIDS, and developing a global partnership for development. Jeffrey Sachs was also primarily responsible for curbing runaway inflation in Latin America in the 1970s. One night, I was on the computer very late doing more research, and I stumbled across what appeared to be Dr. Sachs' direct email address.

This was intriguing, since I've always made a point of reaching out via email to people. Even if they are busy, high-profile strangers, I'll get a response about twenty percent of the time. We hear many horror stories about the dangers and pitfalls of the Internet, but it is a positive tool that comes with a number of benefits. So, I emailed Jeffrey Sachs, telling him that we were several families looking to make a difference and put some capital behind our efforts. I told him that I'd love to chat with him. Fortunately, at this point, I had no idea of his celebrity status, or I might not have made such a breezy offer.

When I got back to my computer the next morning, I had an email from him:

"Call me at 10:20 and I'd love to talk to you."

So, at 10:20 the next morning I called and his secretary promptly got him on the phone. Dr. Sachs and I had about a ten-minute conversation, and then he said "Jeff, I'd love for you to come in to New York and talk further with our team. I'm sorry, I've got to excuse myself right now, I'm in a meeting with the President of Malawi, and I've got to get back into the meeting."

I was blown away and very humbled that this high-profile individual would take the time to spend with us.

A couple months later, I was in New York City with Dr. Sachs at Columbia University. By this time, we'd read his incredibly comprehensive book called "The End of Poverty," and we felt that we were beginning to understand the subject. Dr. Sachs had a group called Millennium Promise that was committed to the eradication of poverty through a different kind of approach. He wanted to "shock the system" by providing infrastructure, schools, and health care, over a five-year period with significant amounts of capital. This was a top-down approach—operating on the assumption that after a five-year period, in the worst of the worst areas of sub-Saharan Africa, if we can eradicate extreme poverty in those regions, then we can cure poverty in any area. He had picked fourteen clusters across ten countries in sub-Saharan Africa and had been at it for a few years already. We eagerly began to learn the details of what he was doing. We felt somewhat in awe as the artist and philanthropist Bono has said before that it is Sachs whose autograph will one day be more valuable than his based on the incredible work that Jeff is doing.

Parallel to that, Mike met an incredible individual through a Young Presidents Organization or YPO event. He's a Canadian named Craig Kielburger, and all you really need to know about him is what he did at age twelve. At his home in middle class suburban Toronto, he was flipping through the Toronto Star newspaper in search of the comics in 1995 when he was struck by a raw and inescapable story. It was about a courageous boy living in Indonesia of Craig's same age who had lost his life while speaking out against child labor. Craig announced to his parents, "Mom and Dad, I've got to go there. I've got to go make a difference."

His parents reacted the way you would normally expect. They said, "Well, Craig, you're 12. You really can't go there."

Craig badgered them enough so that eventually he was able to put together a trip. He formed a group of twelve people at his school, found an adult chaperone, and then they all did a great deal of fundraising. That made it possible for Craig to take a trip to Indonesia with the goal of protesting and learning about child labor. Beyond merely the amazing fact that a twelve-year-old kid was flying off to the other side of the world, self-funded, the trip turned out to be extremely significant for the future of poverty eradication.

As luck would have it, the Prime Minister of Canada happened to be in Indonesia at the same time. When he heard about this twelve-year-old Canadian, he made it a point of meeting Craig and learning about what he was doing. One thing led to another, and Craig started an NGO called "Free the Children."

This organization is about children helping children alleviate poverty. Their schools educate 50,000 kids in the developing world every day. Unlike Dr. Sachs' initiative, this one is very bottom-up. Students in Canada and the United States in elementary schools, middle schools, and high schools raise eighty percent of their funding. They raise these funds both through conventional programs such as bake sales and through other innovative, creative efforts. They're not reliant on large government funding or grants or stuff like that. And the work that they're doing is just absolutely incredible.

Now, fifteen years later, Craig runs the business with his older brother, Marc, a Harvard-educated Rhodes Scholar and Marc's wife, Roxanne. Roxanne is also incredible; she graduated from Stanford and then was also a Rhodes Scholar. The achievement of Craig and Marc is amazing. They are building schools in Africa for Oprah Winfrey. They've won the prestigious award known as the Children's Nobel Prize as well as many other world-wide awards based on human and child rights.

Mike had heard him speak at a YPO event and said to us, "This guy and his organization are going to change the world. We should gather several families and have him speak at one of our houses." Linda, never one to turn away from having an opportunity to cook for people, quickly said, "Heck yes, we are in!" We arranged an event where he would come speak at our home. We wanted him to share his vision with our kids and with several other core families, including the Stone family, Linda's brother David's family and Linda's sister Ruth and her family.

Craig's presentation really resonated with us. He's an engaging speaker, so he captivated all the children in the room—and you have to remember that he wasn't much older than they were. It's exposure to people like this that creates the magic and electricity in their eyes. After his visit, our entire larger family was eager to make a difference in combating the poverty cycle.

Listening to Craig's story that night changed all of us. First of all, he told them, "Look, I was your age and I sat here and I read about poverty in the world." A spark went off with all the kids *and* with the adults.

Then, Craig made a profound comparison that grabbed our imagination. "The United States spends $20 billion on ice cream a year," he said, "and $15 billion a year on perfume. Look, we love ice cream! We don't want you to give up ice cream! And my mom loves her perfume every Mother's Day, so we don't want you not to buy your mother perfume!" The point here wasn't to feel guilty about eating ice cream or wearing perfume but rather to make us all aware that we can solve these historically difficult problems to solve.

During his discussion, we learned several amazingly sad, but very solvable facts. We learned that 4,500 people—90% of whom are kids under 5 years old—die every day from lack of clean water. That's a death toll of roughly one child every 20 seconds. Twenty percent of the world's population lacks access to clean water, and forty percent lacks access to improved sanitation. *Half* of the world's population—roughly 3.5 billion people—have no running water in their homes. The average person in the developed world uses roughly 100 gallons to wash, cook, clean, drink and bathe every day, whereas the average person in the developing world uses just three gallons. Three gallons every day! Any idea what else uses only three gallons? If you guessed one flush of the toilet, you would be right.

Then the big surprise. It would only cost $8 billion to bring clean water to everyone in the world, permanently!

All of a sudden, a light bulb went off in everybody's head: "Yeah, you're right, these problems can be solved!" We knew right there we could make something happen. If we knew what it cost, and we knew what we spend in different industries, then we could be creative and innovative enough to come up with solutions that can help.

He challenged us to come to Africa that summer and see what they were doing, and really understand the difference between "relative" poverty and "absolute" poverty. Relative poverty is "I must be poor, because I can't afford the new iPhone." Absolute poverty is "I live on less than a dollar a day and I walk five miles to get often times polluted water as my drinking water."

Before they even left the house that night, our friends and family were all planning the trip to Africa for that summer. Because Nina had been hearing the stories of the Sudanese refugees as she tutored the kids, she and the rest of the kids were already saying, "We really want to go." Of course, at this point, part of the attraction to the trip was the romance of the whole idea, and their presumption that "We'll get to go on a safari too!"

After all the families left, since his staff was staying at our house, we were up till three in the morning brainstorming about all the different possibilities, getting even more excited. We had already had a trip to Italy planned—a cushy tour to stay at some hotels and sightsee through Italy with our kids. Much to my Italian brother-in-law's dismay, we put that trip on hold and decided to devote a month in Ethiopia and Kenya instead.

In Africa, we connected with three non-governmental organizations (NGO's): Free the Children, Project Concern International and Millennium Promise. Each of these organizations had partnered with thousands of locals in the field, and focused on poverty alleviation, education and sustainable economical development.

The first part of our trip was spent with Millennium Promise in Ethiopia, a beautiful country with extraordinarily beautiful people with model-like facial and bone structures. They use a type of tree bark on their teeth, which gives a spectacular white color. On the Northern Ethiopian border, close to Somalia, we met the most beautiful child any of us had ever seen. Linda desperately wanted to bring her home with us and provide for her. Although Linda wasn't truly serious, when she mentioned it to our oldest daughter, Nina, she said, "Mom, can you imagine someone taking me away from you?" That child is now featured on the home page of the NIKA web site and also on our one liter bottles.

After spending a week in Ethiopia, we set off for Kenya. Marc Kielburger and his wife Roxanne met us as soon as we landed in Nairobi. They were such incredible hosts that they didn't leave our side until we boarded the plane to return back to the U.S. Marc and his team quickly embraced our group. Upon arrival at their campsite in Bogani, Kenya, we were met by their staff and then very quickly by the entire school of kids from Emori Joi, a 500-student school of kids from pre-k through 8th grade. The kids performed a series of songs and dances as the sun set across the beautiful Serengeti desert. These kids had nothing, yet they lived and loved life to its very fullest. They lived well below the poverty line, at less than $1 a day, but they were happy. It was a defining moment for our family to witness their joy.

As our kids interacted with them, Rachel taught the young girls how to play "Patty Cake," while Jacob taught the boys how to throw a football. Nina played hide-and-seek with the kids while Josh competed in running races with them. I turned to Linda and said that I had never felt closer to G-d than I felt in this moment. She turned to me and said this is the way that she felt about her relationship with G-d every day. I was in awe.

On our way back to the cottage that evening, I asked Nina to compare the three different NGO's that we had experienced thus far on the trip and she looked at me with those massively beautiful blue eyes and said, "Oh Daddy, there's no comparison. Free The Children really resonates so much with young people like us." It was at that time that we realized that this was an organization that not only we as parents could benefit from, but also our kids could be inspired by to be the change that they wanted to see in the world.

Through our time with Free The Children, we learned about the cycle of poverty and even did the water walk with girls and the Mammas. The cycle of poverty is directly related to the need to gather water for the family every day, which is primarily the responsibility of young girls in the families in much of the developing world. This is a grueling, difficult and long process. The girls will oftentimes walk 5 to 6 miles twice a day to get water that is oftentimes very polluted. Nina, who was particularly moved by this water walk, says, "We carried the 40 lb. cans on our heads. It was so challenging and difficult. The water we saw was the most disgusting we had ever seen. People were doing their laundry in it. The farm animals were defecating in it. And the people were taking that water home and drinking it. When we came home, we were all shocked."

Because these girls have to get the water each day, they aren't able to go to school. Then because they can't go to school, they oftentimes get married and become pregnant at 12 and 13 years old, then bear children who are borne into poverty and grow up to walk for water as well. This becomes known as the "poverty trap" or the "poverty cycle," as shown in the diagram on the next page.

Free The Children, whom NIKA now supports through donations, now builds one-room schoolhouses that have roofs that capture rainfall and channel that rainfall down into a storage tank. As the water is needed, it is pumped from the storage tank and filtered to ensure its cleanliness. Free The Children makes an agreement with the families of the girls. In exchange for sending their daughters to school to be educated, Free the Children agrees to send them home every day with a jerry can (a fuel container originally made from pressed steel) of clean water every day. While

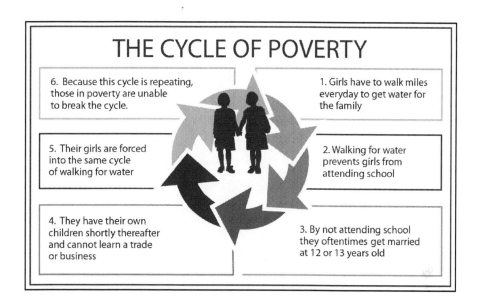

THE CYCLE OF POVERTY

6. Because this cycle is repeating, those in poverty are unable to break the cycle.

1. Girls have to walk miles everyday to get water for the family

5. Their girls are forced into the same cycle of walking for water

2. Walking for water prevents girls from attending school

4. They have their own children shortly thereafter and cannot learn a trade or business

3. By not attending school they oftentimes get married at 12 or 13 years old

the fathers don't seem to care that much about the education, they care tremendously about the clean water being brought home. By keeping these girls in school through the 8th grade and until they're about 16 years old, this system helps these girls become educated instead of quickly marrying and having children, which breaks that cycle of poverty.

As we returned to the states, our family began to digest what we had seen while touring these three incredible NGOs. The kids began to ask questions such as, "How can we help these people?" and "Daddy and Mommy, they shouldn't have to live like that, should they?" We began to think about a business that could hopefully make a difference. But so many conflicting thoughts circled around in our heads. We had to wonder whether we had the patience to begin a startup at this stage in our lives. We'd undergone some tougher times at that point. Did we have the financial resources to see it through? Could we be successful with this business while consumer spending was rapidly deteriorating in this country? The long and short of it was that we were struggling with taking on the risk of starting something new at this stage in our lives. Then we were reminded by a saying in the Talmud: "*Even a poor man living on charity should give charity.*"

◎◎◎

Linda's brother, David Perez, was another example of how ordinary people can do extraordinary things. We all hear the stories of Gandhi and Mandela, we know Mother Theresa, and we know the entrepreneurial nature of Richard Branson. But all of those people remain larger-than-life to the rest of us. We've seen in Craig Kielburger, a twelve year old can make a decision that's going to affect tens of thousands of lives on the other side of the planet. In 2005, David was dissatisfied with the way that society and the government were responding to Katrina and the natural disaster. Three days into it, David just got increasingly dissatisfied. He didn't have a lot of money, but he had a Rolodex and had a lot of "chutzpah." By the time Sunday afternoon rolled around in week one, he had networked his way to people like Michael Dell and Michael Copley, plus a number of senators and congressmen. By the time it was all said and done, he had arranged to have 74 air missions flown in to New Orleans taking medical supplies, baby formula, water and insulin in, and then evacuating people and taking them out. And this was just a guy sitting on his couch getting increasingly dissatisfied with the situation.

Their uncle's heroic behavior was an impactful event for our kids to see. They started to understand the words of Gandhi, who said "We can be the change that we want to see in the world."

At this point, things were starting to come together. We had some capital, and we had these dreams. We had a bunch of dedicated families, including the Perez family, the Tumini family and the Stone family, that wanted to help us and make the difference. In addition, we had lots of nieces and nephews who also wanted to have an impact. We had seen how *ordinary people* can do *extraordinary things*, and we'd seen in Africa how far a dollar can go.

Before long, we focused on the water crisis. *How could we help provide clean water for everyone and safe sanitation for everyone in the world?*

We began to think about creating a company where the profits of that company could be used to bring clean water to those that needed it. The key to us was "sustainability of profits". If we had that, we could pursue many causes.

We also wanted to understand why, with so many well-intentioned individuals and so much money devoted to these problems, no sustainable solutions had been found. We came to realize that many of the world-class people running nonprofits simply did not have great business skills. They were great on the ground with bottom-up, holistic-oriented approaches to poverty alleviation making sure that the critical four components such as health care, micro credit, water, and education were present. But they weren't really good at creating sustainability. For the most part, they rely on government aid, government grants and fund raising. It became very clear in talking to each one of these talented and accomplished people that the one thing that was missing in the NGO world was the concept of business.

Why is the American economy so strong? Because we have so many great business leaders, both of Fortune 500 companies and of small-to-medium sized businesses across the country. But nonprofit organizations often lack individuals with experience running businesses. And without that know-how, they can't succeed in any sort of long-term way. Incidentally, the ignorance is mutual. The for-profits typically don't understand at all what's going on in the non-profit world and vice versa. And we thought that with our product, we'd be able to create a sustainable donation model where just by consumption you could eradicate something.

This is an incredible model because, if it's done right, you don't have to rely on fundraising, grant writing, and other development practices. For example, in the 25 years that they've been around, The Paul Newman charities have donated more than $300 million to various important causes. And that is all through the profits generated from their salad dressings, soups and all their coffees and all their other products. It just became very clear to us that, although these people were talented and smart, they really didn't understand the business side of delivering a service. We realized that since we do understand the business side, we can be a vehicle to fuel all the good that the nonprofits are doing on the ground.

Interestingly, there was a "water" angle stateside also. Linda's brother David had been a part owner of a bottled water company based in Carlsbad, and I was on their board. We began to understand the economics of bottled water, which is that it's pretty darn profitable once you get above your fixed costs. We also learned there's a lot of negativity around bottled water because of the environmental backlash. All those bottles that aren't recycled end up in landfills, and that triggers unhappiness, and rightfully so, among the environmental community. In addition, they argue that the carbon dioxide created during the production of the bottles is bad for the environment, that it's not appropriate to use a scarce fossil fuel derivative for a single-use product like a bottle, and that tap water is just fine, anyway! In short, the environmentalists are not exactly fans of the bottled water industry. So we were already familiar with their concerns.

One of the key moments in the Africa trip was when we did the water walk—where we would walk with the villagers several miles to get and bring back water. It made a tremendous impression on our daughter Nina and our niece Isabella. They connected and understood that the key to the poverty cycle is the walk for water. They saw how it was the women—not the men—who get trapped. These are the same women who are the ones who make everything happen in their village. Our daughter and niece, who both love school, were horrified at the thought that the water walk would prevent girls from getting an education. They started pushing for a bottled water company because they started to realize that it always came back to that water.

Before we left for Africa, we had set up a little test. We made up some paper labels, promoting a theoretical brand of water, and pasted them on some blank bottles. Once in Africa, we showed the prototypes to NGOs and got their response. We took pictures of our kids and the local kids holding these makeshift paper label bottles. Naturally, we actively spoke about the project with our traveling group. Everyone began to get very excited about this idea.

We resolved that when we got back to San Diego, we weren't going to just let this experience, this opportunity, sit idle. We needed to take action and, as Gandhi said, *"be the change we wanted to see in the world."* As we hacked the ideas through and were talking about the different options, it really always came back to water.

In order to understand our decision, a few basics about the water business are necessary to discuss. First of all, water's pure and everyone needs it to live. Bottled water is a $12 billion dollar industry that, as we just mentioned, happens to be under significant attack by environmentalists. Further, more than 60 million disposable bottles of water are consumed every day. We thought: *what if we could couple together a premium bottled water product that donated 100% of its profits with an environmental approach that we believed was best in class for bottled water brands? By doing this and offering a product that tasted good and was priced competitively we envisioned, why wouldn't consumers switch their buying behavior to NIKA?* We came up with a tagline: "Helping the world never tasted so good". Why wouldn't people want to do that?

We didn't have to own the entire market. With just a sliver of the bottled water industry, we could be a $10 million company. We could be a gnat in the marketplace with just one thousandth of a share of the industry, and still be highly successful. We knew from our prior study of the bottled water industry that ten million dollars revenue would generate about a million dollars in after-tax profits. Remembering that it only costs twenty dollars to bring clean water to someone for a lifetime, you can do that math yourself: a million dollars in profit divided by 20 dollars means that we could effectively impact or save 50,000 lives a year. And, if we did that over 20 years, we could impact a million lives.

In addition to the strong social-economic argument, we had an additional motivation. We wanted to teach our kids, our nephews and our nieces and other young people about business—the right way. Our daughter had shared with us that out of her class of 120 high school juniors, she didn't know one kid who wanted to go into business. It wasn't because they're against business, but rather because they didn't think business was cool.

Even at age 17 now, Nina says, "I have very few friends who are interested in business. I wish more kids knew about what social entrepreneurship is. Living with entrepreneurs, I know how exciting it all is. You take a lot of risks, but you make a lot of cool discoveries. You can make money as a business and also help the world with your business."

We needed to make business cool. The entrepreneurial side of our business certainly would be very cool and very engaging to young people. We felt that if we could teach kids the entrepreneurial skills necessary, we could create an enthusiasm towards business. As you well know, at the end of the day, half of those hundred and twenty high school juniors are going to end up in business. So giving them basic skills and a positive attitude about it made a lot of sense.

Finally, there was the question of greed. We found the simplistic rhetoric in the media—"business is dirty, business is just greed"—to be extremely counterproductive toward building a better world. Like everyone else, we'd get emails about the greedy business world, the greedy capitalists, and we'd think, "Oh my gosh, our kids have got to learn a different perspective!"

Of course, greed *is* everywhere—everywhere where there is no morality. If you don't practice capitalism with ethics, of course you're going to have greed. The economic meltdown of the last few years proves this point all too well. At the same time, free markets and capitalistic societies gave all of us the opportunities to achieve what we have. If you take that understanding away, you'll get a whole generation of kids that really believe business is evil or greedy. Pushing back on this mistaken notion was one of the reasons, after a lot of thought, that we chose to make our water venture a for-profit versus a non-profit company.

It's difficult to pinpoint an exact moment when we decided we were *definitely* going ahead with NIKA. But a good indication of our seriousness was this: on our return from Africa, we hired Vividminds, a professional marketing firm to refine our primitively designed bottle labels. The result was a real work of art. They looked so beautiful to us and to practically everyone who saw them. It also may have laid on the promise that we made to Free The Children to help spread the great word about their programs and the work that they were doing.

The excitement increased as we presented further programs in our home to family and friends. We put together a montage that was donated by a brilliantly talented video guy named Randy Stubbs, featuring the family trip that we did with Free the Children. In addition to Marc Kielburger who came back and spoke, we met Anna Trzebinski and her husband, who is a real African Masai warrior. The kids were riveted as the warrior made a presentation in his traditional clothing.

All of our guests stayed with us for a couple weeks. We finished the montage and we put together a guest list to expose more people to the nature of our trip and the activities of Free the Children.

The evening of this next, more elaborate presentation, after all the guests left, we were back at the kitchen table. It was around midnight, we brought out all the food again. That's when we decided, "We're moving forward with NIKA. We're definitely going to do it!"

For entrepreneurs like us, a momentous decision to embark on a large, ambitious project like this always requires a "gut check." There comes a point where you're standing on that high board, blindfolded, wondering if there's water in the pool below you…and…should you jump or not?

At the same time that we were "on the high board" with the NIKA decision, we also had to face a dramatically changed situation with our business and finances. The business we had taken on after the successful sale of a prior company was now having a lot of trouble. Our personal wealth had eroded markedly in a decade due to all our giving natures, experiential group trips, and the other very exciting activities we had sponsored. Understandably, we had some mixed emotions. First, there was the exhilaration of the creation process. But at the same time, we had to wonder, "Are we going to have to sell our house and cars to pay for this?" And if we did try and then we did fail, what would we tell the kids? Our main concern was being able to continue paying for our kid's education. When we moved several years earlier we made a promise to our kids that they wouldn't have to move schools again.

Fortunately, friends and family came through to share the burden. Mike Stone and his family agreed to fund half of the costs and be our equal partners. And Linda's brother David offered to contribute his contacts and his knowledge of the bottled water industry. Ruth's husband, Al, offered to help us with the legal work and Ruth herself was always there for support. Debbie also dove in with all of her creativity to constantly inspire us! We still had one missing part, which was someone to champion the product seriously and sell on a door-to-door basis while also delivering the product. We didn't want to hire someone we didn't know to do this critical function. Linda suggested her godson, Jordan Mellul.

Jordan was living in New Jersey and had demonstrated an insatiable work ethic over the years through working in a rough and tumble South Street, Philadelphia t-shirt and jewelry business. Jordan says, "My dream job or goal was never to work for a certain company or be a certain position. It's always been that entrepreneurial spirit." And his entrepreneurial spirit sure is unmatched. When asked about the key to social entrepreneurship, Jordan says, "Don't say no. Get up and get it done. That's all there is to it. No compromise. No failure. And no surrender. You just go at it every day and believe in it all the way." A young, energetic entrepreneur with a charitable spirit, Jordan was exactly whom we were looking for.

Jordan had participated in our original brainstorming process, so we talked with him about coming out to be the General Manager of NIKA to oversee the day-to-day functions and micromanage our logistics. As

Jordan puts it, "Jeff needed someone half his age and twice his energy to run NIKA." He was inspired to take on the challenge, and a week later, he had moved to San Diego and was living with us.

Since working with NIKA, Jordan now says, "I love that I don't sleep well. I love that I work 24/7 and don't even have weekends off. If I get a call from my teammate in the middle of the night, it's important." That work ethic and spirit is something we couldn't have even asked for from a right-hand man.

By then, our nieces, nephews, extended family members and the Stone clan were all stepping forward to help in whatever ways they were needed. Then Jordan's move and enthusiasm set the stage for our big launch. The NIKA story was about to begin.

CHAPTER 3

Pouring It On

In a start up company, you basically
throw out all assumptions every three weeks.
– William Lyon Phelps –

*W*ITH A PRODUCT WE believed in and had successfully "test-marketed" on friends and family, we now faced the dilemma that confronts every entrepreneur: How do you achieve visibility and market penetration starting from zero, with a limited budget and in a highly competitive marketplace? In this chapter, we'll discuss some of the experiences we had trying to establish our brand. As you'll see, not everything we did worked out, but that's to be expected when you're launching something new.

Making the challenge even more complicated was the fact, unlike a conventional "for profit" company, we were defining "turning a profit" as only the first milestone, not our end goal. As we discussed in the previous chapter, our goal was to create a sustainable source of income, not for the owners of the business but instead for the NGOs that would be providing communities in developing countries with clean water.

Since resources were limited, we wanted every promotional dollar and every minute of labor to be spent in the most efficient way to promote both the NIKA product and the NIKA message. Our first efforts involved getting the product into the hands of a specific group of end users: those who would share our goals and be enthusiastic enough to talk about the product with their friends.

In our first eighteen months, we took the calculated risk of directing inventory and staff resources into several hundred street fairs, farmers markets, and other live events, mostly in Southern California. Results were uneven, of course, but you never know what will work until you try it. An added benefit was that within our team these experiments created a sense of unity and shared enthusiasm, so that we could celebrate the wins together and laugh off the losses. With so many events happening, the planning and management of NIKA became an integral part of our daily personal lives. In addition to everyday school life, holidays, and birthdays, NIKA was consistently a focus of family attention and discussion. Nina now says, "We're a very closely knit family, so I can't imagine a future where NIKA isn't a large part of my life. My career may not be NIKA, but it will always be a huge part of my life."

Finding other talented people to help propagate the message is also so critical. Early on we met two incredible young women, Mila Fisher and Kara Kubarych. They were seniors in high school at the time but you would never know it. During our first summer they managed a group of much older college interns. To watch these two young women do their thing was inspirational in itself. Getting other people to want to talk about the brand and share the positive energy is so critical to overall success and brand establishment.

One of the early street fairs that we did was an event called Fiesta del Sol in Solana Beach, just north of San Diego. This was basically a community fair with music and vendors, but skewed heavily towards the youthful, natural lifestyle. It was a hot and sunny June weekend—which is how we like it at NIKA. These kinds of days are generally when people want to buy a lot of bottled water. Fortunately, our booth was located right next to the dance stage. Everyone was having a good time and it really was one of those magic moments when everything came together. People were into the product, and into the cause—and they really needed the water!

While Fiesta del Sol was a lot of fun, we also worked hard. Josh and his cousin Isaac did a lot of the lifting and moving of the cases. At one point, I had to send them out to get some ice. Soon, they were gone for almost an hour. We were desperately needing that ice and wondering where the heck they were. Finally, they returned, looking disheveled. Each had needed to carry a couple twenty pound bags a considerable distance. When they lamented the difficulty of the task, Jeff told them, "Well, that's kind of like the girls in the developing world, except they have to carry *fifty* pounds and they have to do it for five to seven miles. So how do you guys feel about that?" They got the message.

Other glitches have been less inspirational. All members of the team have had those draining moments, such as when we've been working the booth at a street fair or farmers' market at maybe five or six in the evening. It's misting and the marine layer is coming in. It's way too cold for anyone to want water, and we're standing there just wondering what the heck we've gotten ourselves into. So it's not just about making good business decisions. It's about maintaining your own morale and the morale of the people on your team.

One key way to grow a startup business is what we call "little experiments." If you try a little experiment and it doesn't work, it doesn't blow up your business. Of course, if you do too many little experiments that don't work, you can blow up your business. It's a question of balance. It's always a push-pull between members of the team who want to put on the brakes, and those of us who want to put a bit more on the accelerator. It's a good natural tension because if we didn't have people holding us back, we would have spent a lot more money so far.

If you do enough successful "little experiments," good things will happen. One experiment at a health foods show led to an even somewhat bigger experiment a few months later in Joshua Tree. In March, 2010, we went to the Natural Foods Expo West in Anaheim. We bought the cheapest possible booth available, which put us in the basement of one of the five event buildings. What we lacked in budget we made up for in energy. Other booths were elaborate, multi-floor presentations. Some of them employed professional models to attract attention and push their product. We were in the same little 10 x 10 booth that we use for our street fairs and farmers' markets. Despite all this, we had tons of youthful energy around our booth —and it was contagious.

The energy played a key role in melting the skepticism of our booth visitors. They couldn't figure us out. The typical question that interrupted our NIKA pitch was: "If you donate one hundred percent of your profits, how can you stay in business?"

After a few hours, two gentlemen came by, standing outside the booth, reading the information, and asking a few questions. After hearing the pitch, they got very excited: "This is it! This is it! We've gone through this whole entire building to find you guys! We've found you! We need you! You need us and we need you!"

Now it was their turn to pitch. The two men explained that they were part of a group that runs a big annual yoga event in California's High Desert called Bhaktifest. One of them had attended Woodstock, apparently, and he had no hesitation in describing his own event as the "Woodstock of Yoga." We were immediately interested, but what eventually pushed us over the edge was when we found out that the event was going to be held in Joshua Tree in early September. It doesn't take a rocket scientist to understand that being in Joshua Tree at that time of year is like standing on the Sun! Average temperature is in the 110 degree range. And just for the record, anyone who tells you that "dry heat" isn't as hot has been out in the sun too long!

The promoters now had our interest as they explained that NIKA was exactly what they'd been looking for: this type of water bottle with its eco message plus a social message. They said that they were so excited that they were going to go find their big boss and bring him down to speak with us. This made us excited, because we thought the whole festival sounded pretty big—a yoga festival in the middle of the desert for five days. Surely, the Bhaktifest guests would be drinking a lot of water. But did they already have free water available?

The men returned with the boss, plus a girl in a flower print skirt who looked like she was time transported directly from the sixties. The boss was very reserved, looking us up and down and judging our booth. Finally, he said, "I think this could work, I think this is what we've been looking for; I think you boys have done well."

That sounded good—but when the flower girl started handing us a bunch of papers to sign, we sensed that the whole conversation was going in a strange direction.

Of course, the first two guys had been directing the conversation in a certain way because they wanted us to be a sponsor. That meant that they wanted us to pay to be the only water company at the festival. They started their pitch, and as soon as we heard we had to pay, we became very concerned. We explained that we were a new company, and our goal was to make money so that we could give it away. We told them we would think about their offer. The response was, "Well, we need to know today." They were pressuring us, they said, because they had to make a decision and it had to go in all the literature and signage.

Naturally, we had some concerns about promoting our product in a Woodstock-type environment. We wondered if it would be good for our image if this festival had an unhappy ending. We had heard recent news reports about the cultish New Age "sweat" tents in Arizona where people had tragically died. We just didn't know if this Joshua Tree event was one of those weird things or if it was the real deal.

Fortunately, we had some expert sources to give us a quick read on the situation. Mike and his wife are really big-time into yoga, so we asked them to do a little research about this festival from their friends and their sources. They reported back to us saying, "This is pretty legit, it sounds like something you should consider." So we started calculating: if they're saying they get that many people, it may be a very good marketing tactic for us to introduce a whole new group of customers, mostly from the LA area. So we made the decision to sign up.

As the date of the event got closer, Jeff decided that he had to go up and see it for himself. So he drove up to the festival site, which was literally out in the middle of a field in the middle of nowhere. Given that it was 110 degrees, we knew people were going to be thirsty and we knew we were going to have to keep it cold with ice, so it became a pretty big logistics deal. His first thought was, oh my God, what have we gotten ourselves into? We had just spent about $5,000 sponsoring this and had to buy an ad in their newsletter. It's going to take probably six of our people for three or four days to be up there to make it work. What have we done?

Despite our exclusive deal, we were surprised to learn that we did indeed have competition. When they were pitching our involvement, they had told us that the free water would be out of the way, by the sleeping area. Despite their promises, we could now see that that the free water was set to be fairly close to all the action.

The whole objective for us at the event was a branding opportunity: if we could just break even for the weekend by selling enough water to cover our cost, we could introduce NIKA to between three and five thousand people. Even better, we were counting on the organizers to go back to their yoga studios and use the product there. As Jeff reviewed the site, he realized that our goal was pretty unlikely.

In this case, his skepticism proved unfounded. The event turned out to be a blast. While the free water they gave away definitely affected our sales, that water sat in a large storage tank that had the sun beating down on it. As the days would warm up, the free water would get very hot and our sales would surge.

The festival-goers happened to be a very eclectic group and very earthy. It wouldn't have surprised us if some were on drugs or whatever else that made them act awfully strange. Or maybe that's just California for you! By the end of the fourth day, we saw a few women walking around topless. People were giving stuff and "love" away free! It was a fun event and one that we hoped would lead to increased brand recognition back in L.A. As we looked back we felt extremely happy that it was in fact a success!

◎◎◎

To get a startup brand to that "tipping point" where the internal momentum takes on a life of its own, the entrepreneur has to make daily choices about how to allocate focus and resources. Often, an entrepreneur is forced to make quick decisions about matters outside of his core expertise. An excellent example of this rollercoaster of expectations and realities was our experience with something called "Gifting Suites."

More than fifty years ago, gifting suites started as a way for brands to get their products in front of celebrities attending a prestigious event like the Academy Awards. The brands would pay for the opportunity to be in a gifting suite and the celebrity would walk through a room of twenty or so brands, picking up free merchandise with no strings attached. In the early years of gifting suites, the merchandise was remarkable, i.e. Rolex watches, Tiffany's jewelry and much more. As time has gone on, the "A" list celebrities tended to give away their gifting suite opportunities to friends or family, and, if you're lucky, you get a "B" list celebrity to pass through and pick up the free stuff.

Right around NIKA's nine-month mark, we were invited via our L.A. sales rep to get behind the scenes at *Dancing with the Stars*. The hope is that by giving a certain type of product to these celebrities, they will amplify your message by speaking about it. Neither of us were really very celebrity oriented, so the whole concept did not easily resonate with us. Nonetheless, we figured, if it will help us get the product out there, why not? Clearly, if we could get a celebrity to endorse or support NIKA, it could really be a brand developer for us.

We generally like to try lots of small dollar experiments to test out certain concepts. For the "mere" investment of $5,000, we could test out this gifting suites concept. Guardedly, we said yes, and we were off to the races. Of course, what we did not fully understand was that we had to buy a gifting suite banner, donate additional product and deliver it and much more. So the whole thing cost a lot more than five grand.

The experience with *Dancing with the Stars* was good, and for a pretty low cost. We did in fact get a number of "B" list celebrities to take an interest in NIKA. That was flattering and exciting. We took lots of pictures with them and NIKA, and had our newly-purchased NIKA gifting suite in the background. Did it result in any increased business? Unfortunately not. The average "B" list celebrity doesn't exactly influence people's buying decisions. They just take the free stuff and head for the valet (no limos for them!). The whole thing turned out to be a distraction from what we needed to be doing, brick by brick building our account base.

Unfortunately, because of our initial success, the distraction got even bigger. After what we thought was a decent first start, the gifting suites company owner told me that he had a deal of a *lifetime* for NIKA. He said that, because of our philanthropy, he had gotten support from his team to offer NIKA a fabulous "friends and family" deal.

Were we really that gullible? Heck yes! They offered us to be in their gifting suites for the Grammys, Oscars, Golden Globes and Emmys for the miniscule price of $10,000.

Being an entrepreneur is so difficult. You are always tempted with crazy opportunities like this. On the one hand, most would look at this opportunity and say, "No way I'm going to dilute my focus, that's a crazy investment!" On the other hand, those of us who are dreamers might look at this and say, "Wow, if Angelina Jolie or Oprah happens to show up and take an interest in NIKA, this could be the 'brand maker' that we've been looking for!" There's a decent amount of "dreamer" necessary to being an entrepreneur, but spending too much time (and money) on dreams is one of the reasons that people lose their focus as they create their startups. There is a "reason" that 90% of all start ups fail!

These high-end gifting suites turned out to be a real waste of money. What we hadn't realized was that these suites do not take place at the event. Unlike *Dancing with the Stars*, where we were actually backstage handing out water to show participants, the gifting suites for the major events occur offsite, weeks before the event. Since the gifts are no longer Rolex watches and the like, the A-list celebrities never show up. Basically, they just hand it off to their assistants or someone else. So you end up spending a bunch of money, giving away a bunch of product, all without getting much momentum in return.

So what's the lesson of the "gifting suites" experience? We can't emphasize enough how important it is for an entrepreneur to critically evaluate the expenditure of *every* dollar. This experience turned out to be another business and life lesson learned! And beware of the person whom you meet who wants to be your best friend right away and who promises you the world. Usually, if it sounds too easy and too good to be true, it is!

CHAPTER 4

Carrying the Water

If you want children to keep their feet on the ground,
put some responsibility on their shoulders.
– Abigail Van Buren –

ONE OF THE GREATEST personal benefits of the NIKA experience has been watching kids—both our own and others—learn about business, sales, and entrepreneurship at a very young age. We believed that it was critical for all the kids in the core NIKA community to learn how to make a NIKA sales call. They needed to get their thirty second "elevator pitch" down and even be able to pick up the phone and speak to anyone. An elevator pitch is a critical tool to have in one's bag of sales tricks. By way of example, an elevator pitch for a technology person would be what are you going to say if Bill Gates, the founder of Microsoft, happened to step onto the elevator with you and you had 30 seconds to give your pitch before the doors opened and you had to disembark. It must be incredibly concise and to the point. You've got to be able to deliver on demand and know it cold.

One great example was with our daughter Rachel, who was eleven at the time. We were doing a demo at a large health foods store, where we got people's attention by offering them free bottles of water. Here, you have about five seconds to give that pitch before the person walks away. Once, when Jeff had been away for just a few minutes, he returned to the demo booth, attended at that moment only by Rachel. She said that in these few minutes there had been one couple that had heard her give the

NIKA "pitch". About 20 minutes later, Jeff was alone at the booth and a woman came by and naturally he started to give her the elevator pitch. He didn't get too far when she said, "I've heard it already. Your daughter gave me about two minutes worth of explanation of what NIKA was, about how you're carbon neutral, and how you donate 100% of your profits. She was just dynamic, absolutely awesome, so I don't need to hear any more from you."

That's really the kind of win we like to celebrate: that our child would have the knowledge, skill, and self-assurance to speak persuasively and passionately to an adult.

When we first launched NIKA our ten-year-old son Jacob also came through for the team. Since real life experience is always the best, we decided to train him to sell NIKA on a real phone call. Once we felt that he was warmed up and excited, we tested Jacob by having him call our neighbor across the street. We were much more nervous than he was as he went through the pitch. Jeff says that twenty times during the brief call he wanted to jump in and take over for him! Imagine: here's a ten-year-old boy, selling to an adult man. Eventually, Jacob got to the critical point where he asked our neighbor turned sales prospect for the order. When the guy said, "Yeah, I'll buy five cases," we were even more excited than Jacob! There's a deep sense of joy and beauty in teaching your kids entrepreneurial management skills. Also, the incredible fun that can be generated by doing something with your son or daughter.

Building the brand also required that we create a hard-working ground game effort of customer acquisition, which we call "direct store distribution." Our reps needed to build up the brand by going up and down the street, visiting restaurants, coffee shops, bagel shops, nightclubs and coffee places and making the pitch. You don't necessarily sell a lot of volume in these kinds of places, but you can quickly build up consumer awareness and build your brand name. To really create the sales volume, however, you do that through natural foods retailers. In all selling environments, you need the right price, and the product has to be attractive.

When we started the company, our cost per case of water was high. Our cost was definitely higher then what you could buy the lower priced commodity waters for. Over the first year, we were able to lower our cost by about 25%. That's all good, because the lower pricing allows us to compete very effectively in the premium of the bottled water market. But it's very difficult to compete down low against Kirkland, Costco's brand of water or Crystal Geyser or Arrowhead, or different commodity waters where all you've got is just the water itself. You don't have a story, and you've got a very inexpensive bottle and an inexpensive label.

Early on, as we mentioned, we opted to go with a label that was a little more expensive, in the hope that it would grab the consumers as they walked by in the aisle. Since we don't have millions of dollars to spend on advertising campaigns, we had to make it very viral—so that the product almost jumps off the shelf by itself. That's one of the early things we did very well.

The label is so colorful that people oftentimes say, "Oh, I love that bottle! I was walking down the aisle and I saw this colorful bottle and it really jumped out at me." Even though our products may cost more, we felt like it was an important trade-off early on to make that value proposition very significant for the consumer and grab their attention. We knew we were on the right track when, in a completely different context, a woman told Linda, "I purchased these stunning NIKA bottles and I just cannot get myself to throw them out. I have them all lined up on my desk. I have them lined up at home. They're so beautiful."

Linda told her that she could do what a lot of people do and use them as flower vases. She thought that was a great idea. Another friend of ours bought one case, but now she just refills it with her tap water and carries the bottle around! That's not good for sales, but it certainly is an endorsement of our packaging.

For the most part, we have a very low customer turnover rate. Typically, when a customer doesn't come back, it tends to be something like that fact that they bought the water in a liquor store that really doesn't care about the social message at all. We've learned to narrow our sales focus to the types of accounts that work for us, and the types of areas that work for us.

By December 2009, we realized that we needed to establish a presence in the natural food channel—large retailers such as Whole Foods, Jimbo's, and Henry's. They are different than typical grocery stores, which tend to offer products at a lower price point. Natural food stores tend to attract the organic-oriented consumer, someone who desires to be educated on the pluses of different types of product, and is typically willing to pay a little bit more. A more premium product like NIKA fits in this environment, because we can tell the message about our social cause, and the message on our eco approach. But we didn't really know how to get to the natural foods channel.

Fortunately, we came in contact with a super gentleman, a "beverage consultant" named Jim Tonkin—the kind of person who Malcolm Gladwell, author of *The Tipping Point*, would classify as a "connector." Jim is the kind of guy who knows just about everybody in his industry. He was exactly the kind of person we were looking for and needed.

In each of the different businesses we've owned or operated, Jeff has always tried to identify the person that's really in the know and well-connected in that specific field. These are the people who, if they like you, your product, and your value proposition, tend to be willing and open to connect you to their contacts. For a new brand, these kinds of connectors are invaluable.

Jim came out to our house and we spent a day with him talking about how to build this brand and how to get it to the next level. He said the natural foods channel was really the right direction for us. When you go to the natural food channel, you typically go to a distributor, in our case United Natural Foods Incorporated, or UNFI. You sell the product to them and then they resell it to the natural foods retailer. In fact, they don't actually sell the product—they technically take title, and they do the actual selling and delivering to the stores, but they aren't going to pitch it to the natural foods retailer. We have to do that ourselves. The problem was that we don't have the necessary relationships to get in front of buyers.

We also had to hire a food broker. Jim recommended a few people who we talked to, and the one we hired was a group called Presence Marketing West. We hired them just for California, but they have a national footprint. The good thing is, as we grow, we can have them assist us in other cities and other areas. To start, we decided to keep distribution limited to California. That's because you have to pay the food broker a commission, but there's a minimum charge per month. All pretty normal, however, another investment cost for us to digest!

We began to work with Presence Marketing West, who then introduced us to Whole Foods, Jimbo's and to Henry's. Jimbo's was an early adopter and a great friend to NIKA. Although they are just based in the San Diego area they have a very loyal customer base who cares about organics, causes and the environment. We then were able to begin to get Whole Foods in gear, so one of the big positives last spring was when this prestigious store agreed to take our product. Whole Foods is really important because they have a national footprint. If they wanted to, they could take us national overnight. They seemed to really like NIKA, but they had to make sure that the product would move and could generate the "turns" (restocking the item at a store because it is selling well) that they hoped for. Even though the natural foods retailers all love the cause and the eco messages, they need to run their business in a profitable manner. It's important from their perspective, so it's important from our perspective, too, that we get the product out there and that we make actual sales to consumers. Otherwise, if we don't, they'll take the product off the shelves and we won't grow. Jim helped us get the food broker, and that helped us get into Jimbo's and Whole Foods.

Once you're into these different places, the great thing is that now you have an answer, at the street fairs and farmers markets, when people ask where your product can be found. It's difficult to say, "Well, it's in Joe's Coffee Shop" when they may not live anywhere near that business. But if you can say (in Southern California), "It's in Henry's" or "It's in Whole Foods or Jimbo's," most consumers will know about it, and that really helps to legitimize the brand. Legitimizing your brand is critical. You always want to make it look and feel bigger to the consumer than it is. So that happened over the course of the second six months from our launch date.

After we got into the natural foods channel, three large potential customers came our way. At some level, each was a bit of a wild goose chase. But the selling experience helped us tighten our cost structure and refine our product pitch. The Carbon Fund, which is our carbon credit organization, was so impressed with NIKA that they talked about us to the Ritz-Carlton, which was looking for a water supplier. The hotel already gave away free water in their rooms, but they were looking for a higher eco profile. When we made our pitch to be their exclusive supplier of bottled water. They loved NIKA and they loved our green approach, our social cause, and the looks of the bottle.

The challenge became our cost structure. They already were supplying guests with purified water with the Ritz Carlton name on it, but we could not compete on a cost standpoint. They were using a very inexpensive bottle, plus an inexpensive label. We didn't get the deal and for a while, we were heartbroken. It was a great experience for us nonetheless because it forced us to go back and really push our costs. Additionally, it forced us to perfect a marketing outline, an overview that we would use to go out to new buyers.

We weren't effective in getting the Ritz, but we pressed on, connecting with a fast growing chain of quality health food restaurants called Panera Bread. They have 1,500 retail locations, and we thought this was going to be a great branding opportunity. Through informal family connections, we were able to get to the founder and have him learn about NIKA. He was impressed enough to connect us with Paul Saber, the local franchise owner who owned about 35 units in Southern California. When we met with Paul, we immediately hit it off, in part due to our common interests and passions. In addition to his success at Panera, over the years he's done tremendous work through the Billy Graham Foundation, as a significant contributor of theirs. Throughout the world, he's been working in poverty alleviation by building churches, schools and many other things. When we met with him and introduced NIKA, he immediately said, "Look. I've got a different brand. But I'm willing because of the cause to switch to NIKA if we can get the cost anywhere near where it needs to be."

So for a number of months we really worked hard to try to get the cost down for Panera. In the end, though, we couldn't quite get it to where we needed it to be. Nonetheless, we developed an incredible relationship with Paul. He still wants to get us into Panera, but we haven't been quite able to get there yet because it's a function of the cost and some other issues. We were talking about a co-branded label with Panera, and NIKA, and we're still struggling through that process.

At the same time as we were working with Panera, our NIKA sales manager, Dave Musil, was independently following up on a cold call to Tully's, which is a Starbucks-like coffee shop retail chain. As it turned out, they were about to make a franchise water decision for fifteen of their southern California franchisees. Dave just happened to step in there on the right day at the right time. He was able to get a meeting the very next day with the head buyer for their Southern California region. As difficult as the Ritz and Panera were, Tully's basically made an immediate buying decision to switch to NIKA. Tully's turned out to be an incredible account for us because they present the product well and they talk about it well, along with their coffee product. They allow us, and encourage us, to do demonstrations at their stores and giveaways at their new store openings. We're hoping that over time we can develop a relationship to get into all of their Tully's 250 stores throughout the United States.

Also around this time we got into Baja Fresh, an upscale Mexican fast food restaurant chain. Again, the chemistry just clicked and Baja Fresh was as easy as Tully's for us to get our product in. Since then, they've both been really good accounts to us.

We celebrated our one-year anniversary in March 2010. We had been building the brand through an on-premise customer acquisition model, which meant going up and down the street to individual stores, knocking on them door by door. Now, we had also developed a channel with the natural foods industry where we were beginning to get some traction. Our start up plan was to focus on Southern California and make the model work here before we took it elsewhere. But at about this time, Jeff had the opportunity to do a speaking engagement on social entrepreneurship at Harvard. We discovered that when you can go out and do these speaking engagements, it reinforces the brand. It gets people enthusiastic, and people want to help the cause. Jeff went to Cambridge and spoke on social entrepreneurship. By the end of the presentation, people were really taken by the NIKA story. Several came up to me afterwards and said, "Hey, we really love what you're doing; we'd really like to help you launch the product here in Boston."

We thought about it a little bit and decided that a distribution effort in Boston would be great, even though it is a long way away. For our marketing focus, the Boston area with its 375,000 students was perfect. As we've already noted, NIKA resonates with young people because they tend to really focus on environmental and social causes. In addition, we thought that when these young people go home during the summer, they could take their knowledge of NIKA with them back to their hometowns.

So we said sure, if you want to help us get some merchants over the summer that would be great. In addition to Kara Kubarych who was now a freshman at Harvard, we had three additional people over who helped us that summer: Tony Wang, Dian Yu, and Sebastian Garcia. All three were in the presentation that day, and each promised right there that they would allocate a portion of their summer to assist NIKA.

The trio went out and started cold-calling merchants. We told them that once they start to get some merchants going, we would find a distributor for Boston. The best shipping option was pretty obvious. If you buy an entire truck from point to point, your transportation rate is the cost of the truck. If you don't have a full truck, then you do what's called "less than truckload," or "LTL" and the rates are significantly higher. So the only way the deal can make sense is if we can ship it at full truckload, and the only way that makes sense is if we have a distributor there that can take the delivery. The standard distributor typically has a whole range of different beverages and product that they take to their street locations. We spoke to a few, but we weren't really getting the attention that we wanted. A few of them sent draft contracts—all wanted very onerous terms. For example, if we ever wanted to separate, we had to pay them the equivalent of a year's worth of sales back to them. That's because they're all fearful that after they build up their client's brand, the client will sell it to Coca-Cola, and Coke will then to take the product to its own distribution channel. Even though some of the contract restrictions were understandable, it just didn't feel right.

Parallel to that, Kara had gotten an account called Ackers Vending, a small company with about 50 vending machines on the Harvard campus. She spoke to Louis Fiorenzi, the owner, who was so taken by the product that he said he wanted to meet the owner. We quickly got on the phone with him, and we could tell that he was a super nice guy. He told us that he wanted to help, and that he wanted to put NIKA into his vending machines on the Harvard campus as the sole water in those machines. He took care of that, including making sure that there were placards with the machines explaining how NIKA donates its profits and our eco methods.

We were struggling with finding a distributor, and at the same time we really liked this guy Louis. We figured that maybe we could do something creative here, an informal agreement, without a contract. We proposed to him that we ship a truckload of water, basically on consignment. Basically, we would absorb the working capital costs and put the product on the shelf for him. Then, once a month, he would take an inventory of what he has left, and we would invoice him for that and he would then pay us. He would actually ship to the merchants that we get signed up in the Boston area. Louis said yes—and it worked. Sometimes the "industry standard" isn't the only way to get things done! Being an entrepreneur is oftentimes all about being flexible and thinking outside of the box.

The arrangement worked. Louis does the distribution, and charges us a twenty percent margin, which is cheaper than what a traditional distributor charges us. He doesn't have the cash tied up in the product. And he bends over backwards to drop cases off when we want to do demos. We created a real win-win, and the beauty of it was that Louis and NIKA did the contract with just a handshake. This was particularly impressive as we live in society that almost always requires twenty page contracts for just about everything. Louis told us that his wife said, "Louis, how do you feel about working with NIKA? Aren't you worried about the risk of getting stuck with product?" He told her, "Look, this is a great company, we have no exposure. We have a handshake agreement, which I love and you don't see in this day and age, and we only have to pay them when we actually sell the product." Louis and his organization are just super salt of the earth people.

This creative approach to a tricky distribution situation shows how important it is, as a startup, to be both entrepreneurial and flexible. We're now at the point where we're looking for a full-time person to work with Louis. We have campus rep programs going at other Boston area schools to drive demand for the product.

While that idea worked, the simple truth is that not every concept will turn into great success. To backtrack for a moment, soon after NIKA's launch, we created our own sales concept called the Agents of Change (AOC). The idea behind it was to adapt the "Girl Scout cookie" model to selling NIKA water. We hoped to motivate kids—elementary through high school—to take orders for selling NIKA. We would deliver the product, and then the seller would earn AOC points for how much they sold. Instead of getting an award related to personal gain, the points would be redeemable for what we call "charity rewards." For example, with a certain level of points, they would be able to bring clean water to someone for a lifetime, or donate a well in someone's name in developing world. For more points, they would be able to win a trip to go help those schools somewhere in the developing world. When we kicked it off, we had high hopes that this would be a great program attracting a lot of participation. So far, it's only turned out to be an "okay". We have shifted our focus more to the younger grades. You're not going to hit a home run every time!

At the same time we got NIKA going, we were the sponsors, along with Project Concern, of the annual Walk for Water in San Diego. The whole day, people were walking to simulate the walk for water that people do in the developing world. They carried five-gallon pails filled with water on a 5K walk. With this difficult walk, people got just a little sense of that whole concept of absolute poverty versus relative poverty . We donated $25,000 to be a sponsor of that project, and one hundred percent of the money would go to building wells in a particular project. The first year, that project was in Nicaragua. And as we did the water walk, we of course had NIKA there and we publicized our projects. Heavy rain fell all day long, which made the walk even more arduous for the participants.

It was a success for us nonetheless. A year later, a group of us was fortunate enough to go to Nicaragua to actually turn the water on for the first time from the wells our money had paid for. It was really a powerful, transformative moment. Along with CEO of Project Concern, George Guimaraes, we took some of our children, plus a bunch of their schoolmates who had been involved in planning the Water Walk. We flew into Managua, and then we drove kind of a bumpy road for about 6 hours up to the northern border of Nicaragua. From there we went up on a full-day trip off-road that was really in the middle of nowhere to where these villages were. In this particular small village, people were living at the top of a larger mountainous area with no water. They were forced to walk down two miles to the bottom of the valley to fill up with dirty water that was polluted from runoff from other villages. They would then take this dirty water back up to cook, clean, wash, and drink.

There was water on this mountain from rainwater, but the people in these communities had no ability to access it. With our financial donations, Project Concern drilled into the side of the mountain and created a big concrete vault that captured the rainwater. From there, they piped it through a gravity feeding system of PVC pipe down to two different water towers. From the water towers, they took it to several schools, health care clinics, and then one hundred different homes.

As we left the village in a covered wagon on a bumpy road, we had a funny experience that let us know the trip had made a deep impression on the kids. One of our NIKA sales guys, Nick Kubarych, began to get the group singing songs, and they were exchanging words, putting the name NIKA in for different familiar songs. One of them was The Beatles' "Let it Be". But instead of singing the refrain "Let It Be," they sang "Make It Clean!" To us it meant that the authenticity of the poverty alleviation experience—and the tangible improvements we could make—was sinking in. It's one thing to read or hear about a situation, but to experience it in person is much more powerful. The knowledge and enthusiasm that our crew absorbed on the Nicaragua project translated into a whole new level of meaning and enthusiasm when they spoke about NIKA to someone else. That's why we always try to take people to our projects.

Later that day, we returned to the village where they had a little celebration for us when we turned the water on. It was a big deal for the community, because now all of a sudden they could really transform their lives. They now had fresh, clean water at the school, the health care clinic, and in their homes. The whole community came out; it was almost like a 4th of July celebration. We did a ribbon cutting ceremony at the school. Just seeing the faces of the people, so happy that they had water, and our NIKA team seeing the impact that that could really make, we knew we were doing something profoundly meaningful. We were demonstrating the fact that business really could make the world a better place.

CHAPTER 5

Riding the NIKA Wave

The tipping point is that magic moment
when an idea, trend, or social behavior
crosses a threshold, tips, and spreads like wildfire.
– Malcolm Gladwell—

*T*HE RACE WAS ON: to accelerate brand awareness at a rate exceeding normal consumer momentum and get to a "critical mass" status before we ran out of money. So the challenge was how to create what author Malcolm Gladwell calls a "tipping point", where momentum takes over and you have a successful brand that you've created without spending a fortune.

Our general consensus was that you couldn't necessarily *force* the tipping point. What you *can* do however is effect the environment around you by making it conducive to a tipping point event. It's very similar to how we understand individual success. When you hear about somebody that got really lucky, if you peel back the onion, you discover a person who most likely spent his career focused on developing specific talents and skills. Then, when an opportunity arose, he "got lucky." Jeff often says that opportunity is the meeting of preparation and luck. A company needs to be similarly positioned to grab its own luck.

A key indicator that you are approaching that tipping point is when evidence appears that your message has gone viral—that the promotion of your product has taken a life of its own. That's why, with a limited promotional budget and no established marketing team, NIKA's marketing focus needed to be on the so-called "social media" tools such as Facebook, Twitter, and YouTube. Also, email blasts can promote similar viral excitement—both from purchased lists and from names we gathered at NIKA events. Any or all of these tools can quickly and inexpensively help get the word out. For example, we created fifteen fun videos about various aspects of NIKA. Jordan, our handy general manager, also spends much of his time setting up events and investing in our public presence. Every day, more people see these things online—and you never know whom you are going to influence.

Basically, the key to getting to the tipping point is to place the product in the hands of what Gladwell calls "connectors". We've spoken about Jim Tonkin, who was our connector in the natural foods channel, introducing us to people and companies up and down the chain. Similarly, we needed connectors at the consumer level. These are the people who would be able to know and understand the NIKA culture, and then talk about it for us. We learned that, as a team, we could be pretty effective finding these consumer connectors. Sometimes, the key to identifying these people was to simply put free water in the right person's hands. We tried to place NIKA in on-site locations where potential NIKA connectors would go—the right coffee shops, burger shops, and clubs.

The NIKA culture is really a youth culture—both at the delivery and the consumption end. The average age of our personnel was in the range of twenty-six years, providing the energy and enthusiasm that launched the brand. In a startup, you work a tremendous amount of time and you put a in a great deal of energy. If you're not really motivated, you're never going to be really good at helping the brand get traction. When we met Dave Musil who is now our sales manger we clicked right away. Dave graduated form Harvard and wanted to live back on the West Coast. He's also been quite involved in charity work through his surfing days. While money is important to Dave, he's clearly more motivated by doing good deeds and giving back to mankind.

In a startup, everyone must be willing to do the necessary heavy lifting and groundwork. For example, in his own words, Jordan's daily tasks as General Manager involve "making sure that the product is ordered, the website has enough information, our trucks are maintained and our deliveries and accounts are all up to date," but we joked about the fact that he was also one of our main delivery drivers.

We agree with Jordan when he says, "Everyone is aware of their roles and works at breakneck speeds. They put in 150% all the time, every time."

Often, one of our sales reps, Eric, would be delivering the product in his NIKA t-shirt and jeans. Then, he'd be back the next week for a sales call. Our customers would react by saying, "Oh my gosh, I didn't know you were a salesperson. I thought you were a delivery person." That's what a startup is all about. Another interesting example was when we met Eric Bach to discuss him becoming a sales representative, we had a hunch he would be a good fit. Eric had been with a nonprofit organization, so he immediately understood the concept of what we were doing at NIKA. Eric was also working three jobs as a bar tender and the thought of working for a stable company and earning a commission based on new account acquisition was very enticing to him. In Eric's case, as with most good sales professionals, a strong incentive was very motivating.

Throughout the earliest days of NIKA, we found we were governed by what we called "The Rule of Two." A startup takes twice as long as you would expect and costs twice as much as you would budget. That's just the essence of practically any endeavor. It's human nature to possess unbridled optimism about a new project. Even if you try to check that optimism, you tend not to think about *all* of the costs associated with accomplishing your goal.

When we started NIKA, we had hoped we'd be at an operational break-even by the end of the first year. Now, just starting our third year, we hope to be at a break-even rate by the end of *this* year. The company's growth is taking a little bit longer, but that's an inherent part of creating a brand.

We *do* have options. If we went into a "prevent defense" right now and stopped investing money into the product, we could quickly get a lot closer to our financial target. But that would mean holding back on our PR, on the website, and in broadening the geographic sales footprint. If you choose to invest in your brand, you have to understand that the decision is going to affect your cash flow.

In order for NIKA to achieve its social goals, it must first meet some important financial milestones. First, we must become a million-dollar-revenue business in Southern California and break even in Los Angeles, Orange County and San Diego. Once that's achieved, we will then use that as the vehicle to provide the sustainability the company needs to do its philanthropic work. Until we really get into that break even, NIKA will remain a costly venture for us. For the NIKA project to succeed, we knew that every aspect of our organization would have to reflect the company's special mission. As we began our run at the "tipping point", we had to make choices across a full spectrum of business challenges. Every aspect of the NIKA project required decision-making that reflected the values of our mission. For example, let's take a look at staffing, production, and marketing.

—Finding the Right People—

As we built the brand, we were really careful to look for people like Nick Kubarych—knowledgeable, friendly, and willing to fulfill enthusiastically a wide range of job assignments. We also had to be sure that as a team we really gelled, because that's where you can generate the magic of the entire enterprise.

Jeff remembers one of his early performance reviews at the beginning of his own career. One of Jeff's bosses told him that he was too close to his managers and in effect was a "friend" manager. Further he was asked to separate from his team a bit. In fact, though, we *do* think it's important for managers to sincerely like the people who work for them. You *should* be able to go out and have a soda or a beer with your associates, and have their families over for dinner. Hopefully, the feeling is mutual, and the employees for the most part like *you*. This perspective has been really important to both of us throughout our respective careers. When you break down these social barriers, business is not only more enjoyable—it also creates the environment for people to want to jump through walls for you.

—Motivating Our People—and Keeping the Pipeline Full—

Selling—both to smaller shops and to the larger stores—requires a dedicated, hard-working sales force. Fortunately, the NIKA mission attracts exceptional people who are very capable of doing a great job. The question is this—at a time when we don't have a lot of money to pay people, how do you get these great people and how do you motivate them?

To address the challenge, we came up with an innovative compensation structure for our NIKA sales reps that allowed us to reward achievement while preserving our limited capital. We were paying these really talented associates a base salary and a commission based on new account deliveries. We wanted the commission to be as high as possible so it would be motivating. We were all about customer acquisition versus making money on the first sale. Our strategy worked: once we implemented the program of aggressive commissions, business increased about four hundred percent. We went from about one hundred customers to over four hundred customers in the first year.

For NIKA to grow, we needed rapid account acquisition. Because of the investment that we were making in the brand and the environmental campaign, we hoped that this would make the product "sticky". This means that—once the retailers got the customers to try the brand—those customers would continue to request it. In fact, that has been the case. As long as NIKA remains sticky at the retail level, we will continue with our current sales commission plan.

As we got better at this, we began to understand that account acquisition was a bit of a science. Imagine a pipeline where you've got new customers at different points on the spectrum. Some are at the "end" of the pipe, ready to close. Others are in the middle; these are the ones where our sales reps are already talking to the owner. Finally, there are the potential customers we're identified via the cold calls on retailers.

We learned that you need activity at all three stages. If you let the pipeline go dry at any point, then you're going to have a dry spell for however long that period continues. It's vital that the sales reps are active in all points on the pipeline, including making those cold calls. Keeping the pipeline full is sort of a "Sales 101" concept. But we've applied it in our own way to NIKA, and it has helped build the brand.

One of the first critical items in the NIKA project was the development and positioning of our product line. We started out with a single item, the half-liter NIKA bottle. Of course, we knew that we needed to have a liter product, and we needed a six-pack product. If you can sell a store multiple products, then you can double or triple the amount of business you do. Already, we had a number of customers who would tell us "Gee, we would love to add your product line, but we really don't want to have half a product line of NIKA and half a product line of Fiji." They said that once we had the liter product, they would give us orders for both. So, in those early months, we began to develop the two new products.

Another critical area that got our focus was *product cost.* Compared to the commodity waters like Aquafina, Dasani, Arrowhead and Crystal Geyser, NIKA is a higher cost product, competing much more on the lines of Fiji, Evian, Ethos, and Smartwater. The key reason for this pricey market position was our cost structure. Even if the starting cost difference might not seem great, by the time you add margins from manufacturing to retail, the price will be a multiple of four or five times that original cost. So, if you have a dollar cost, the product will resell for four to five dollars. As a manufacturer, it's not that you are making all that more. Mostly, it's going to essential outside components such as distributors, brokers and transportation. One way to lower costs is through volume production. Another is through investigating and then optimizing the cost of each step of the process. Then, because you can now lower your price in the market, you've expanded you potential market size.

Sometimes it's effective to lower the price temporarily. When we wanted to quickly increase activity in a specific store, we would hang tags on the

NIKA bottles that said "Buy one, get one free." This would of course entice new consumers to try the product, and also increase the volume that the store was selling. Price promotions can get expensive, but they will often build customer loyalty.

Next, we had to rethink our labels. Our son Josh said it didn't make sense: *Why were we considering spending extra money on fancy bottle labels when the whole point of NIKA was to get the money to the communities that needed it?*

He was right: we wanted to push down costs and thus have more money to give away—but we also wanted our product to stand out and communicate the NIKA message. Just like our brightly colored giveaways such as NIKA t-shirts, a high impact bottle label could help us create a brand and hopefully also capture the attention of people long enough for us to discuss awareness of the water crisis.

About six months in, we had the design people at Vivid Minds come up with a new label, which was extremely colorful with fewer words. Our original label contained much verbiage on the front and back, mostly in small letters that were difficult to read. The revised label communicated a brief message in a large font: *NIKA donates 100% of our profits and we're eco-friendly and carbon neutral.* Most people can now read our label without squinting or looking for their glasses. The new labels *did* increase our cost structure slightly, but we believe it was well worth it to elevate awareness of the brand understanding of our company mission.

At the in-person demonstrations, we quickly saw the effect of the new labels. Now, many more prospects would pick up the bottle, read our message, and admire the art. At subsequent farmers markets and street fairs, we would commonly get comments such as "Oh yeah, I saw NIKA a while ago. I loved the graphics so much that I've saved the bottle and turned it into a vase." We always like the sound of that!

There is also an amazing story of connecting the dots behind the beautiful portraits that are the faces of our labels. Years earlier when Jeff climbed Mt. Kilimanjaro in Tanzania he was captivated at the base of the mountain in the town of Arusha when he saw the amazing art work of Stephen Bennett, aka "the Portrait Painter". Stephen uses really vibrant colors reminiscent of the paintings of Andy Warhol. When we decided to start NIKA, Jeff spoke again with Stephen Bennett and asked if he would be willing to donate his artwork for the labels. After Stephen learned of the great social cause of NIKA, he gladly agreed. His assistant, Victoria Graham, was also integral to reaching this agreement.

If NIKA were just a simple water company, then building the website would not be terribly difficult or expensive. But we had a multi-faceted message—first about the product, then about the mission of the company, and then about the opportunities to be *part* of that effort. Our website would have to be elaborate enough to explain all that, plus it had to be visually interesting and colorful to match our packaging and our promotional items. We knew that our consumers wanted to be aligned with companies they perceive as vibrant and growing. With proper design and content, the website could also inspire them in that direction. We are continuing to add content, which communicates new and different aspects of the NIKA story. All good websites are always a work in progress, including ours. Since we couldn't spend much money on advertising, the website was a cost-effective allocation of our promotional dollars.

We are constantly looking for innovative ways to promote our brand that cost less but have greater impact. For example, in the approximately 150 demos and appearances that we did in that first year, many were promotional events for philanthropies. In lieu of writing a check, we would donate the water. The charities loved it; if it were a dinner, they would put a bottle of NIKA at each place setting. We tried to choose events that promoted causes that were like-minded to NIKA. That way, the attendees would be people more likely to be interested in our story. The great thing about the bottles as we designed them was that they functioned as their own advertising. Just like the retail experience, when you pick up our bottle for the first time at a charity event, you immediately grasp that NIKA is eco-responsible and donates all its profits to poverty alleviation.

One more way for a startup to get around the prohibitive cost of paid advertising is through free publicity. Early on, we hired a public relations firm called JPR to assist our own efforts. They placed us in a number of local newspapers and also helped us get featured in Entrepreneur Magazine. The professional fees we paid were fair market value, but in the grand scheme of things they were very inexpensive. A published article about NIKA from a third party can be much more authentic and thus more powerful than simply buying an advertisement.

We tried to do as much public speaking as we possibly could. Our first face to face was at Wellesley College in January 2010, when we were invited to speak at the Madeline Albright International Development Conference. A close friend had attended the school and was able to bring Jeff in, on a panel with three other speakers. As he told the NIKA story and showed one of our videos, the message really resonated with all of us. Afterwards, the majority of the panel questions were directed toward NIKA. Following the formal discussion, a number of people lined up to ask us direct personal questions about the entrepreneurial startup model and NIKA.

The second speaking opportunity was at Harvard in the spring of 2010 to a social entrepreneurial conference. We probably had only 75 people in total, and Jeff was one of a number of speakers. A few months later, we again spoke at Harvard at a social innovations conference. That led to the development of our Boston student sales force, which we've already discussed.

In August, 2010, we spoke at Georgetown to a group of 250 MBA students. We were the fourth keynote speaker of the week, and the professor was pleased by our presentation. He said that each day the speakers got a little bit stronger and that we had really tied together the concepts of leadership and social entrepreneurship.

Back in California, even our kids became active speakers. Nina, Josh and Isabella appeared in many schools at all grade levels. Eventually, Nina also had an opportunity to speak at the World Water Conference at Emory University in Atlanta. Each appearance was an exciting opportunity and the kids always stepped up to the challenge. As the official NIKA youth spokesperson, Nina now travels to various conferences to share the NIKA story and educate others about the water crisis.

Nina says, "I was always comfortable speaking in front of groups. My dad and I do a lot of the speaking together. He'll cover the business aspects, and I'll cover the more humanitarian aspects of it. It's really been a family affair and it's fun to play a role in the company with all my other siblings."

—Linda adds—

I don't do any of the speaking. Jeff and the kids do it all. When Nina or Josh or Bella have to speak, I get very nervous on their behalf. I wonder: *how are they going to get up in front of a room of these college kids and make an impression?* But they know the subject matter well, and they're passionate about it. It always blows me away how beautifully they do and how incredibly well they're received. As a parent, it's really an amazing thing to watch.

One of the neat things about doing a business with your kids and other young people is that they learn to develop their own voice. That's such a great part of growing up. It pushes kids out of their comfort zone to maximize their talents.

When the kids speak to a very young audience, they have to make sure to communicate at that level. Last year, Nina spoke to a group of elementary school kids. You can't do a PowerPoint presentation to a group of first graders—you've got to make it real and very experiential. Nina was able to have individual different kids stand up and act as continents of the earth, differentiating between those that have access to clean water and those that do not. Then, she had a couple first graders walking around with a pail of water to show the kids how heavy it was to carry. Naturally, until now, these kids had no understanding of this other world, and it made a big impression on them.

Little by little, we found that our guerrilla marketing approaches were working. At the beginning of a speech by Robert Haggett, CEO of *Newman's Own* food products, Jeff asked for a show of hands if they've ever heard of NIKA water. Probably 200 of the 260 people raised their hands. That was the extent of the market research we do at NIKA! But it's still very encouraging when you get feedback like that. It makes you believe that all the hard work brand building, all the early mornings standing at chilly farmers' markets, are paying off. You realize *the NIKA concept does work*, and that it's just a question of time before we can achieve our next set of goals.

Like most other startups, we wanted to branch out into other products and expand the footprint nationally. In a perfect world with unlimited funding, we would have already have hired a half dozen people in key geographic areas. We would already have direct sales people spread out, and we'd be hiring distributors. But instead of doing all the items simultaneously in parallel, we are choosing to cautiously open up these markets one at a time. We wanted to do things quickly, but we also wanted to do things the right way and stay within our budget. And as far as we could tell, we were!

Part Two

The Next Wave: Social Entrepreneurship

My best object in living is to unite my invocation with my vocation.

– Robert Frost –

Get the free mobile app at
http://gettag.mobi

CHAPTER 6

Reflections on Year One

Learn from yesterday, live for today, hope for tomorrow.
The important thing is to not stop questioning.
– Albert Einstein –

EVERY STARTUP HAS SPECIAL challenges and a social entrepreneurship venture even more so. As the company approached the end of its first year, we reviewed where we'd been financially and where we were going. Many entrepreneurs hate fiscal self-examination, particularly in the early phases of an enterprise. Nonetheless, a serious and professional analysis is vital— while there's still time to make course adjustments. Even though we're a cause-based company, at the beginning the entrepreneurial startup factors are more important than the philanthropy. That's because if we don't get the business right, we'll have nothing to donate! So we needed to take stock of where we were.

Roughly speaking, NIKA's early efforts were weighted four parts business to one part cause. Over time, once there's sustainability, we expect to flip that ratio; NIKA should function as four parts cause, one part business. Until then, we have to resist the temptation to let the cause projects pull our hearts. Sometimes it's better just to hunker down and make the business successful first. People don't really understand that even though "cause" and "donations" are the 100% objective, we need to build the bridge with good sound business fundamentals.

We sell a high-price product into a commodity industry, not unlike selling BMWs in a world of Chevrolets. How do you justify the higher price of the Roadster? The Impala and the BMW each has four wheels and will get you where you're going. Each has different features and benefits. If the customer perceives that the benefits he desires are roughly equivalent in both vehicles, then he is probably going to purchase the less expensive choice. BMW's marketing challenge is to illuminate that differentiation.

Similarly, NIKA must define its uniqueness in a manner that the consumer readily understands. Right out of the gate, our competitors in bottled water have a significant advantage. Most of them don't use the combination of being carbon neutral, using post consumer recycled plastic to make the bottles and don't repurchase bottles to mitigate the impact on landfill. Moreover, NIKA is a high-priced product entering the market in a recessionary economy. There's already downward pressure on the price of a bottle of water, and there's increased green pressure in a lot of communities to get rid of bottled water altogether.

All of these obstacles can be overcome by educating the consumer that NIKA is a superior purchase, more in line with their personal values. Once people understand our eco-message and our social agenda, they generally respond, "Oh, okay, that's pretty good." But if they remain unaware of the NIKA difference, the product never gets a start.

For most people who want to start a business, whether it's in the dorm room, at the kitchen table, or anywhere else, a key challenge is finding the necessary startup funds. The NIKA experience shows that, while undercapitalization can be fatal, the temptation to spend limited resources too quickly is equally dangerous.

There are multiple ways to grow a business. You can hit it with a lot of cash and try to accelerate the growth through the impact of your purchases. But, if you do, then you run the risk of being unaware of problems in the underlying model until it is too late. With too much cash, people tend to waste that money. For better or worse, every dollar that we spend as a family on NIKA is one less dollar that we can reserve to make sure our children can safely get through college. It's important for our own discipline both as a business and as a family to make sure that the dollars we're spending are directed wisely. Whether you've got a million dollars in the bank or just a thousand, you still need financial discipline. Great ideas that run out of money are nothing more than great ideas!

We talk to people all the time who tell us that they don't have a lot of money to start. We respond that their predicament is not necessarily a bad thing. If you don't have the money right now, you should develop your dream—on paper—as a business plan. While you're working for someone else to pay the bills, you can make mistakes and learn on their nickel. Then, when you're really ready to take that leap of faith, you can jump off.

If you approach family and friends for funding, remember that you can usually only go to that well one time. Before you do, make sure that (a) if it doesn't work out you're not going to affect your relationship, and (b) you are *really* ready—because if you mess it up because you weren't ready or because your model wasn't right, or you spent too much money (we call it "dumb money") too fast, you're *definitely* not going to be able to go back for a second time.

The problem with a lot of venture capital deals is that the individuals they are funding have visions that aren't necessarily based on underlying economic realities. As an accountant by background, Jeff generally takes a conservative approach. You've got to make the model work before you can really double down and invest heavily on that concept. Otherwise, you will quickly burn through your resources.

In the example of NIKA, if we went out and tried to raise venture capital money, then maybe we could accelerate the plan—*but at what price?* We would have to give up either the authenticity of our vision or the control of the brand. Instead, as we've discussed in the previous chapter, we're taking a bit longer and building the company brick by brick.

Judging your own startup's balance sheet can be painful. You're often acknowledging the fact that you either didn't generate as much revenue as expected or you spent more money than you expected. Nonetheless, it's really important to do this "post-mortem" on a quarterly basis, semi-annual basis, and annual basis. That's the only way you'll understand what activities are not working and what you should continue.

For NIKA, in the beginning, it was really about establishing the revenue line on the balance sheet. We knew that, over time, we could lower our cost. We also knew that an initial ramp-up of spending would have to occur just to get a business off the ground. The real question was: *is there a real business here—and can we generate revenue?*

In our second year, sales revenue was about 350% higher than what it was in the first year. So we've proved that the venture does have revenue potential. Plus, we're lowering the product cost by 25% this year, just by getting more efficient and increasing the volume. We're not repeating some of our money-wasting projects, so we know that over time we can lower cost even more. But if you don't have the revenue, none of this cost-cutting really matters.

Managing cash flow also requires self-honesty. Keeping in mind the "Rule of Twos," you just got to look at a venture and say, "What do I think this is going to cost each month?" and, "What am I prepared to spend on this in total?" It's really important to closely measure cash flow because many people look back all of a sudden and complain, "Oh, man, I spent ten times as much money on this as I was going to," or, "This took me ten times as long!"

As we prepared a year-end statement and began budgeting for our second year, our partner Mike Stone retrieved the three versions of the budget that we had prepared a year ago: a better-than-expected, an expected, a less-than-expected. Then, together, we reviewed the possible outcomes that we had envisioned. Looking back a year at our original three scenarios, Mike reported that we were definitely operating *above* the worst-case scenario, but not quite at the *expected* scenario. This was disappointing, but it was important information. If we didn't think through its implications, we would have been setting ourselves up for failure down the road.

We had to keep our eye on the most critical tasks. Knowing that, it's still easy to jump at unexpected opportunities, such as the invitation to expand our geographical area to Boston. If we had been only sensitive to the cost side, we probably would have rejected the opportunity and restricted our focus to Southern California or even simply San Diego.

Expanding more rapidly than we had planned was not a *wrong* decision—but it was a decision to spend more money and allocate more assets. Our choice was based on the assumption of a certain level of incoming revenue—a level that we did not completely achieve. At the same time, our fixed costs did not budge, and we could not spread them over as many transactions as we had expected. Nonetheless, we think we made the right decision in the first year by exceeding our budget when special opportunities arose. While those gains are not yet reflected on our balance sheet, we can all see the contribution our extra projects made toward development of the brand and grassroots promotion of NIKA both as a product and a culture.

One reason our revenue goal was not reached was that we misjudged exactly when we would be able to get the natural foods channel up and running. We totally underestimated the time it takes in that sector to create brand energy. The process is very difficult, and there's a reason why large companies allocate huge marketing budgets for products even if they are already in that particular space. When you're trying to create a brand on a shoestring, it can be very difficult and time consuming. But it can also be a lot of fun, with a great payoff at the end.

The other challenge with a startup is that you don't always get to quit your day job! Throughout the entire NIKA rollout Jeff has also been CEO of a building products company that does several hundred million dollars annual business. Not only was this a full-time job but it was also a business in deep trouble. Virtually no other industry was affected as adversely as the building products industry with the 2009 recession. But NIKA is our passion, and it consumes the hobby time that would normally have been spent reading, playing golf, or doing other sports.

Because of our children's participation in NIKA, this business has allowed us to spend more, not less, quality time with them. As we all know, most teenagers are trying to figure out reasons why *not* to be around their parents. So it's great that our kids, plus those of family friends and in the greater community, have adopted the NIKA cause. This is a positive activity you can do with your teenager as compared to just sitting on the couch watching television. NIKA or similar type businesses are excellent ways to interact with your kids, brainstorm with them, and get their creative ideas while at the same time teaching them some business sense.

The benefits of bringing in our youth extend beyond merely the gratifying sense that we're engaged in good, inspiring parenting. Frankly, one of the keys to a startup business in today's market (unless you have a lot of venture capital money) is that you've got to make it viral. You've got to make your product or cause energize the grassroots, as we discussed with the social media. Getting young people engaged in the process is critical, because they are the ones who are going to tell their friends. Then, their friends are going to see NIKA at the coffee shop and they're going to buy it. They in turn are going to tell their parents to pick it up at the store. They're going to tweet their network or they're going to put it on their Facebook or their blogs, plus on things that we don't even know exist yet. Youth can be a great, low cost contribution to accelerating brand identity.

Managing a startup, you've got to be both a Chief and an Indian. If you're just a chief, and you're not willing to get your hands dirty, you're not going to get your people to run through walls for you on a Friday afternoon at five o'clock. You've got to show them that you're willing to do the heavy lifting too, or they're going to be put in a position where they're going to say to themselves, "Hmm, I don't really have to do this heavy lifting".

Jeff leaves the sales cold calls to our reps, because he believes they're better at it than he is. A prerequisite for selling is the ability to take rejection and move on, and Jeff acknowledges that's very hard for him. A good sales person has got to be able to recognize that for every twenty calls, you're doing well if five of them become serious and you can actually close on two. That's just the law of probability at work there. If that's not your skill set, then delegate cold calls, because the frustration and rejection can really dampen your spirits for the whole project.

Probably a quarter of Jeff's time is spent on actually going out and doing demos, getting in front of the customer, and doing street fairs. We both love the experience of having someone come up to us and then getting to make that five-second elevator pitch. We've also got a twenty-second pitch, and a one-minute pitch. Deciding which pitch to use is all based on reading the person's eyes as they walk by. As you hand them that bottle, you ask yourself, *do they really just want the water and that's it—or are they interested in hearing more than a five-second pitch on what NIKA's about?* If so, you go to the next twenty-second pitch. If, at that point, they're still standing there and they haven't moved away, you launch into the minute=long pitch. But if they're fidgeting, you let them go—because you want them to have a good experience.

Giving out water can be more difficult than it seems, because it goes against people's natural inclination that nothing is free. We once heard a father walk away explaining to their kids, "Johnny, they say it's free, but nothing is free. Don't stop at those kind of booths."

It's such a shame because, of course, we give it away for free, and there is no catch. We do demos at different stores because we want consumers to try our product. But one store encounter is not going to change a potential customer's lifetime of conditioning.

We like the human nature aspect of the demo environment. Because they are unaware that we're the owners of the company, and they don't know that we've had a successful business background, they just think we're employees handing out water. When you put yourself in the position of being the server, you really get to see how people treat other people.

We make a point of treating people the same as we would want to be treated. We always try to treat the janitor the same way that we would treat the CEO. And I'd like to think that our kids do that also. We teach our kids this, because different people will approach us in different ways, and we needed to prepare our children for that reality. Some people will give you an attitude, because they don't know who you are, and others will treat you like they treat their brother. A famous Jewish Rabbi named Hillel once said that the key to all Jewish scripture was one phrase, "Do not do to others what you would not have them do to you."

Probably fifty percent of Jeff's time is spent on company logistical management. He does the ordering for the product to make sure we've got product on the shelves. If, all of a sudden, we run out of product, it could take us four weeks to replenish. As a startup, we cannot run out of product. Can you imagine getting Whole Foods excited about our brand and then saying "Oops, we're empty and we won't have any for four weeks?" At the same time, we can't have truckloads of unsold water sitting in the warehouse, tying up a lot of cash and working capital.

We're big believers in MRP Planning, which stands for Materials Requirement Planning. This refers to a system of demand planning to make sure you've got the components and the supply. MRP is not just a way to make sure that the product is in stock. It's about having the labels in stock, and the empty bottles and the caps. You've got to have the shipping boxes, also.

All those things need to be in place. When you start to drop your inventory, you need to be able to replenish without having to waste time. We spend time making sure that gets done right. To make the task more efficient, we've built little spreadsheets specifically for NIKA and we work off of them to monitor our status.

We also pay great attention to customer relations. Emails take a good deal of our time, many of them coming from our website. Some people will say "I appreciate what you're trying to do but I just can't get behind a company that sells bottled water." We try to respond to all those concerns and educate them on why we chose bottled water. We explain to them how, in fact, we want to be best in class environmentally and here's what we're doing about it. We don't necessarily win all those people over, but we defuse their suspicions. They've probably never gotten an email reply from a CEO before, so that's a positive thing, right?

While we also have staff to answer emails, we make a point of answering the ones that come from students and teachers. Generally, they have an idea to share or they want to help. When they get an email back right away, and it says "from the founder of NIKA Water," they're impressed. They don't know how small we are, and they're simply pleased that we responded so quickly and effectively.

Finally, there's strategy. As NIKA's leaders, we also spend time thinking about the next products, the next generation, and the next label. The world of strategy is about thinking big picture: *where do I want to go? what tree do I want to climb? how do I make sure that I climb the "right" tree in the "right" forest?* If you climb the right tree but in the wrong forest you get to the top only to look around and see the forest in the distance that you really want to be in. Conversely, if you climb the wrong tree in the right forest you get to the top and see many taller trees surrounding you. As leaders we have to always be concerned with fundamental operations: blocking and tackling well (to use a sports analogy) and executing our game plan. If leadership is concerned with strategy at the expense of operations, you can waste a ton of money or stock yourself out of product.

Frequently, you find startups that spend their way into oblivion or they don't have a sense of bottom line. Or, they have a great strategy and they're big picture thinkers, but they can't execute down on the minutiae, detail, and tactical level. NIKA does a good job strategizing what our next goal should be. We also are always thinking about the tactical execution plan on how to achieve that. You've got to keep your head in both worlds. Our balanced approach is one of the things that we do well.

When NIKA breaks even, we'll be able to fulfill on our dream of sustainable funding for water in developing countries. Whether it takes one year or ten, we know we can make a very sustainable donation model. At that point, NIKA will have national visibility. We hope that we will have important media recognition inviting us on their shows because they are so excited about the concept. Whole Foods will get so enamored that they want to offer NIKA throughout their chain. These kinds of external validations can further bring NIKA to that tipping point, where the operation no longer needs to be kept alive through our own funding and energy.

It's fair to ask if we had begun this project five years ago, in more affluent times, would our success have come more quickly? As far as dollars and cents, maybe so. But the optimal timing for the social entrepreneurial experiment is not then, but right now. With everything that the business world is going through, and with the difficult social issues that exist around the world, people are looking for new solutions. NIKA is our attempt to connect American values and the opportunities of capitalism with the ability to make a difference in social programs. We want to make business-building a positive experience that is appealing even to idealists who only want to "do good". That's why right now may be the best moment to introduce the NIKA approach into the world.

CHAPTER 7

How Charitable Organizations and NGOs Benefit from Social Entrepreneurship

For it is in giving that we receive.
– St. Francis of Assisi –

*W*HAT IF SOCIAL ENTREPRENEURSHIPS didn't simply benefit charitable organizations and NGOs, but could help eliminate extreme poverty altogether?

In this chapter, through a number of examples, we'll look at the way that the social entrepreneurial bottom-up approach—the hand *up* versus the hand *out*—is a much more efficient way to address poverty than the traditional top-down-driven, handout.

The most basic purpose of any international development organization is to help lift the poorest people of the developing world toward what's called the "bottom rung" of the poverty ladder. That lowest rung may be ten feet off the ground, but if an individual is able to grab that bottom rung, then he can begin to pull himself up out of poverty. For most of the impoverished people in the world, this bottom rung is out of reach.

Poverty remains pervasive because, for a number of reasons, the Industrial Revolution appears to have sailed right past developing countries—whether in Asia, Africa, South and Central America or elsewhere. Some primary reasons include the absence of innovation in agriculture and the absence of manufacturing. Colonization and corruption also played key roles in holding back industrialization.

Another reason why a developing country might show little progress in its development is an unstable government. When an unstable government is present, private capital doesn't want to come in because private capital is always concerned about guaranteeing a financial return. Unstable governments elicit fear in business people. And when people live in fear, they're paralyzed from doing anything. Throughout most of American history, a lot of people have been willing to bet large sums of money on a lot of other people with great ideas. However, this practice hardly occurs in developing countries because few people trust unstable governments and as a generalization, entrepreneurs don't have proven track records. The problem isn't a lack of trust as much as it is the evidence that this mistrust is actually founded on real numbers. In the last 40 years, the developed world has invested approximately $570 billion in Africa, and yet, Africa's per capita income hasn't changed at all. This proves that throwing money at the situation isn't the answer. We've got to come up with a better solution.

The World Bank's annual "Doing Business" report ranks 183 countries based on the ease of doing business, with 1 being the easiest to do business with and 183 being the worst. Of those 183 countries, only 3 of the top 50 countries are from Africa—Botswana, Mauritius and South Africa. Each of these countries provides a different example for what works on what economic levels. But what separates them from other, less developed African countries are their freer capitalistic policies and their promotion of entrepreneurship.

Thirty years ago, Botswana was one of the poorest countries in the world. But because it changed its system to one in which people have property rights, greater economic freedom and a fair judicial system, Botswana has grown by an average of 10% per year since then. Botswana demonstrated one of the highest economic growth rates on the planet during that extended period of time. Now, Botswana has even attracted outside capital from Hyundai and from Heinz.

Simply handing money to governments doesn't work. It's estimated that for every dollar that the government invests, typically all but 30 cents of each dollar gets eaten up in bureaucracy. So only 30% ends up benefiting the actual investment. Most charities and non-governmental organizations that have higher than a 20% administrative rate have difficulty garnering donations.

In her book *Dead Aid*, author Dambisa Moyo states, "Foreign aid props up corrupt governments—providing them with freely usable cash." Throughout the book, Moyo documents which countries have taken what aid, where the money has gone and what corruption exists in these exchanges. The three African countries that are prospering—Botswana, Mauritius and South Africa—decided not to take aid and instead hold themselves accountable and maintain a free market economy.

When a country implements innovation and free market solutions, its people are better able to hold each other accountable, and a country emerges that is completely different from one that is run by a corrupt government.

A corrupt government is a red flag that inhibits businesses from investing. Businesses typically don't want to invest their assets when they fear that a country will be nationalized or their assets just taken from them in the middle of the night. Corruption not only makes it difficult to do business, but it also makes it unsafe for people to work in those countries. It's a spiraling, downward effect. Investors want to steer clear of this kind of malaise. People in these countries can't plan ahead, because they don't know where money for the future will come from,. And if people can't plan ahead, then economic stagnation spreads, illiteracy spreads, poverty spreads and crime and corruption become an endless cycle. When corruption is present, the people aren't being invested in. And if you don't invest in something, it eventually goes awry. It's therefore no surprise that the World Bank's "Doing Business" report shows that the poorest countries in the world are the most difficult countries to do business with.

In *Dead Aid*, Moyo mentions Erwin Blumenthal, an IMF representative who was posted at the Central Bank in Zaire, which is now the Democratic Republic of Congo. While in Zaire, Blumenthal wrote a letter that said that we cannot do business in Zaire. He said that we absolutely can't give money to this country because it is so corrupt. But as soon as that memo was released, the IMF still gave Zaire the largest sum it ever gave to an African country. Then what happened? Over the next ten years, the president of Zaire kept $700 million of that fund for his own personal use in his Swiss bank account. But corruption is still only a small part of the trouble when giving money to governments. In the past 50 years, $2.3 trillion has gone into developing countries from developed countries all over the world. And that $2.3 trillion has been largely squandered. Most of that money doesn't even get to the people it seeks to help. For example, when the large NGO's in the United States fundraised a tremendous amount of money for Haiti, very little of it actually benefited Haiti. The issue wasn't corruption as much as it was bureaucracy, which didn't let the money trickle down to the people.

If you enter the countryside of many of these developing countries and forget about the government, you can work very comfortably in the rural setting. You can work with the villagers because they're not corrupt. They just try to survive. In order to implement sustainable models through which locals can begin to create more income in their villages or in their country, sometimes you have to go around the governments.

Extreme poverty won't be solved by governments giving large amounts of money to other governments, who are then trusted to pass along large amounts of money to NGOs in a top-down fashion. The top-down approach has been tried and it has failed. What needs to happen now is for non-governmental organizations to create change from the bottom up, starting with the villages.

The African countries that have done this by refusing government aid are shining examples that the bottom-up model works. And they're making these changes on their own. When I heard Dambisa Moyo give a lecture and in her radio interviews, she said that most people in Africa are people of pride. They want to be responsible for themselves, but their corrupt governments keep them from reaching that bottom rung on the poverty ladder.

This is where social entrepreneurial businesses step in.

These businesses provide a way for investors to invest in actual local people versus the government. Social entrepreneurships also allow entrepreneurs who donate their money to pick the charities and NGOs that they want to do business with. The entrepreneur—the individual—can figure out which NGOs are productive and which ones aren't, then hold the NGOs accountable and shift the donation capital accordingly. Governments are less able to do what entrepreneurs can. Governments provide aid at a very elevated level, but they have a difficult time getting to the grassroots level and can't articulate where the money actually goes.

When we donate a dollar to any one of our NIKA projects, we know that the full dollar goes to the specific project and not to administrative costs. We handpick the NGOs, and even within those NGOs, we can determine what percentage of our dollar goes to administrative costs.

We've seen organizations such as Free the Children and Project Concern International successfully circumvent governments. Yes, they have to cooperate and work with the governments on some level, but they don't give money to the governments. Instead, they go right into the villages. They come up with *holistic solutions* to their problems. Holistic solutions require a holistic understanding of extreme poverty. In order to eradicate poverty, we have boiled down four key actions which *all* must occur in order to eradicate poverty:

1. **Fix the body**—with health clinics and health care
2. **Provide clean water**—available close by
3. **Make micro-credit available**—as pioneered by Mohammad Yunus
4. **Education**—particularly for the young women

If you just solve one or even two of these four items, you will not succeed. For example, if you fix the body but you don't bring clean water, then the body's not going to stay fixed. However, when groups take this holistic approach and address each of the four critical areas, they see significant drops in infant mortality, significant increases in life span, and significant increases in literacy.

When charitable organizations and NGOs take a holistic approach to problem solving, they see improvements in "life". The key to these improvements is beginning at the grassroots level from the bottom up. Like we've said before, it can't be a handout. It needs to be a realistic hand up. Engaging with the village and creating sustainability within that village is the heart of social entrepreneurship.

One tangible way to create sustainability is through Bangladeshi economist Muhammad Yunus's concept of micro-credit, or small loans for locals in developing countries. In one instance, a group of women were taught the "merry-go-around" system. Each week, the women get together and each woman puts a given number of coins into the pot. Through a pre-determined system, each week, one woman takes the money from the pot and chooses to spend it on whatever she feels will benefit the community. She can buy a cow or something that will be an income-producing activity. The women hold each other accountable, which prevents anyone from squandering the money. This type of micro-credit system creates sustainability in the village. (Note: it's the *women* who get the money, not the men!)

Eradicating extreme poverty isn't about giving millions to Kenya or to the Congo. It's about entering the villages at a grassroots level and working with the people holistically to alleviate all four legs of poverty. For the most part, even unstable governments are willing to let organizations come in and do that. The main challenge is that if these governments really are unstable, NGOs don't want to put their people in unsafe situations. So step one is working around the current broken system of governments. Step two is getting money to these bottom-up projects.

Social entrepreneurships give NGOs the luxury of time. They provide financial sustainability for charitable organizations and NGOs so that instead of spending two-thirds of their year fundraising or working on grants, these organizations can actually work in the field. Sustainable donation models are important because over the last 100 years, the pattern of donation capital in the developing world has operated on an unproductive start/stop mentality.

For example, let's say that as our family allocates our annual donation capital, we decide that we really like this guy who builds wells in Africa so we support him with a check each year to build the wells. Let's say we do that for a number of years and it all goes well. But then a situation like the 2010 Haiti earthquake or Hurricane Katrina occurs, so we want to reallocate our personal donation capital towards a deserving project where there's been a disaster. Or let's say the recession hits closer to home so we want to tighten our own balance sheet and reduce our donation commitment. All of these situations and changes in donation capital are fine and make a lot of sense, but when we stop writing that check to that well-driller who brings clean water to people in Africa, his project can't sustain itself and it ends.

When you drive through the countryside of developing nations, you discover that they're littered with half-started projects and buildings that may not have been properly planned or may not have had funding to see them all the way through. You see discarded equipment and machinery.

Someone might implement the latest, greatest water purification system in the middle of Africa next to a polluted river. But that fancy system was made in Germany or the United States and requires parts made in Germany or the United States. So the system works well, but when the first part breaks, the entire system is abandoned and is never used again. The best systems seem to be the ones that have buy-in from the villagers and utilize the greatest amount of indigenous parts from the area.

This start/stop mentality is a reality for a lot of NGOs. Unless an NGO has a multi-year government grant, it can't plan long-term in its projects. This incentivizes very short-term thinking for the NGO, unlike the business, which has the ability to create long-term strategic plans. Building clinics, water well systems, schools and orphanages are all well and good, but there are maintenance factors that need to be considered. It's one thing to get the money the first time, but NGOs must have a consistent source of funding, and the most sustainable way to do this is to generate income from within the village.

In developing countries all over the world, you see half-finished buildings and understaffed, rundown facilities because they don't have a source of sustainable capital. It's easier to fund a tangible asset than to fund an intangible program. Some donors tend to care more about seeing an immediate building go up with their name on it than they do about making sure a nurse's salary is being met.

We gravitate to NGOs such as Free the Children and Project Concern—two NGOs that we've worked a lot with—because they make sure to try to create income within the village. Keeping the money in the community is really the answer.

The way to do this is by correctly managing post-processing costs. Let's explain this concept with the example of shea butter, a cosmetic cream that women use in the United States. Shea butter sells for about $8.50 a pound in the U.S. In Mali, in Western Africa, where the shea nuts come from, indigent farmers sell these nuts at what's referred to as "farm gate pricing." Their farm gate pricing is about 30 cents per pound. That 30 cents per pound undergoes several steps through various middlemen and then eventually turns into $8.50 a pound. Everything that occurs after the farm gate pricing is what we call "post-processing."

If we could figure out a way to do some of the basic processing of the shea nuts in country, then we could keep a lot of the economic value in Mali or in the villages of the farmers. This is a huge deal. If we can turn that 30 cents per pound into $1.30 where the sale of the nuts occurs, then the people at the source of these shea nuts keep that extra dollar, which goes right back to the per-capita income. The key to people reaching that bottom rung of poverty is to keep more of the profit margin in their homes.

We already see this happening in a positive way with the coffee trade and the growing popularity of fair trade coffee. Before the implementation of the fair trade certification process, people in the developed world wanted to support farmers, but they supported them at about 30 cents per pound of coffee. At this rate, however, farmers don't receive enough money for anything other than subsistence, so they aren't able to invest in their land and then their land goes bad. This actually occurred in Haiti, where farmers sold their coffee trees to make charcoal because charcoal was worth more than the coffee was worth. Insufficient funds decimated what was once a vibrant industry in Haiti.

Today, certified fair trade coffee beans must be sold at about $1.50 per pound. Fair trade coffee keeps more of the income in country, but fair trade coffee—and especially organic, fair trade coffee—still represents only 4% of the overall coffee market. Still, it is a step in the right direction.

In addition to keeping more of the profits and income in country, NGOs and charities need a better solution for sustainable donations. We'll give you two examples of social entrepreneurs who've found this solution.

In the early 1980s, Paul Newman started making salad dressing for his close friends around Christmas time. He noticed that around February, those same friends would ask him to make more of that salad dressing because they liked it so much. Newman began to realize over time that people really did enjoy his salad dressing. Then at some point, a light bulb went on and he realized he could make this salad dressing, package it and sell it.

Because he had done well in his life as an actor, Newman didn't want this to be a profit-making business. So he decided to allocate the profits to different charities that he supported. The company—Newman's Own—migrated into soups and pastas and a whole line of products that, as of August 2010, had generated about $300 million for over 650 different charities. Newman's Own now gives away about $25 to $30 million a year in donations.

We've modeled NIKA after this model of sustainability for the NGO world. It allows the recipient charity or the NGO to focus on what they do best—to address their causes and not worry about the time-consuming and difficult process of raising money.

Our second example involves two men—Mike Hannigan and Sean

Marx—who were also enamored of the Paul Newman story. In 1991, they were both working in the office supply business. When their company was acquired, they could choose to stay and work at the acquired company or go and do something on their own. They wanted to make a buck, but they also wanted to implement a version of what Paul Newman did. So Mike and Sean created an organization called Give Something Back, an office supplies organization in the Bay Area that has now donated approximately 75% of its profits—about $5 million. Mike and Sean also let their employees and their customers pick the charities they want to donate their products to. Today, Give Something Back has over 12,000 clients.

Partly inspired by both of these stories, we created NIKA because we saw that the for-profit models created sustainable donations. We abide by Mike and Sean's belief that if a company can prove that its product doesn't cost any more and can benefit the community, people will buy the product. Through something as simple as the consumption of a bottle of water, which occurs in the United States more than 60 million times a day, we believe we can draw enough people toward NIKA so that they can help make a difference in the world. *We only need a sliver of these daily consumptions to save thousands of lives.*

Because there still aren't as many social entrepreneurship examples such as Newman's Own and Give Something Back, there is still resistance to for-profit donation vehicles. But it's important not to vilify capitalism and alienate an entire group of people who might be financially motivated but also want to contribute to the world's greater needs.

In Muhammad Yunus's book *Building Social Business,* his tag line—"The new kind of capitalism that serves humanity's most pressing needs"—shares many similarities with what we're talking about. His premise, however, is that capitalism is the root of our problems. Yunus argues that CEOs with capitalistic mindsets and for-profit mandates can't think socially because they're afraid of shareholders kicking them out of the CEO seat. This mentality has, in turn, caused an optimization of profit at the expense of everything else. So Yunus espouses the idea of a benefit corporation, in which the investors of this corporation—a for-profit business that donates 100% of its profits—legally agree to getting back no financial returns. The investors will only get the money they initially invested.

We come at this very, very differently. Besides the cause itself, what fuels the heart of social entrepreneurship is the entrepreneurial spirit. A benefit corporation looks too much like a non-profit, for us. If we took the profit-seeking motive away from social entrepreneurship, we'd lose a large percentage of people who would want to do this kind of business, but also have a desire to make money. We'd lose the Give Something Backs of the world.

It is important for the person who wants to implement a startup to be able to make a buck on it. And if that person can also make more than a basic wage and actually have an upside to work for, then that person might work harder because it means something to his or her wallet. Not everybody is financially motivated, but there's no reason to cut out a huge group of people who are.

Our business philosophy is that a social entrepreneurship should have some giveback component to it—whether it's 25%, 50%, 75% or 100%. We chose 100% because we had the ability to do so. But if you are starting your own business and you want to donate half your profits so that you can have your feet in both worlds—we believe that that is also a very laudable, positive model. The clothing line Jedidiah donates 5% of its revenue to a different charity every six months. Since they started doing this in the mid 2000's they have donated more than $450,000. Everyone can utilize a different model but merging the for-profit business with a non-profit component is inspiring to all!

Give according to your own capacity. Every individual has a different capacity to give. Many successful businesses didn't give back any percentage of their profits when they started out. But they gave back in different ways, by employing people, creating jobs or setting up scholarship funds or helping their local communities in a number of ways. To paint the business world with a broad paintbrush that says business is evil—we think that's wrong and unfair. We fundraise with our children's school and we approach our local businesses all the time. They support us and donate to our gala once a year.

If you're Bill Gates and you can give $26 billion, more power to you. But if you're a college student on scholarship and you want to be valued as part of the community and your giving capacity is $10 to give to an organization, then participate. Give your $10 proudly.

Too many people say, "The bigger guys will take care of it so we can sit this one out," but that attitude doesn't solve anything. Everybody needs to give to his or her capacity. Adopt the same philosophy when creating your business. Identify a giving range that you're comfortable setting up and give within that range.

The United States doesn't always have the proudest history when it comes to developing countries. But there are no utopias on this planet, and to its credit, the United States always seeks to better itself. In our country, we like to face our problems, deal with them and move on. We catch our Bernie Madoffs and we execute justice. The United States also possesses a strong entrepreneurial spirit that, if directed properly, can propel the changes the developing world needs. There are too many NGOs and charities that are self-focused and intent on realizing their individual visions. Too many of these organizations try to solve only one of those four aspects of poverty. What we need are more organizations that can be holistic in their problem solving.

A bigger issue is that too many NGOs are run by people who come from NGOs and not by people who come from the business world. Oftentimes they don't consider concepts such as post-processing or microloans. We need to pair America's entrepreneurial spirit with its heart, so that organizations are more efficient in providing that hand up instead of the handout.

This spirit can be found everywhere in the United States. A man named J.B. Schramm began a non-profit called College Summit. While in graduate school, he worked as an academic advisor at Harvard and counseled kids in high schools to get into colleges. Schramm found that in lower-income areas, the shining stars of these schools were already getting into college, but there existed an entire middle tier of lower-income high school students who didn't go to college even though they weren't the bottom of the heap.

Schramm worked with colleges to open up their standards to this whole middle market and then rallied different non-profits to help fund scholarships for these students. He started in 1993 with 4 students. Since then, he's gotten over 40,000 students trained and into college—students who otherwise wouldn't have gone to college at all.

Another example is Better World Books, which collects and sells used books online. The company donates the money it generates from its sales to literacy projects. Since it started in 2002, Better World Books has donated more than $7.5 million to literacy and education. Just from collecting old used books.

These examples aren't theoretical. These stories exist in the world and yours can, too. So how do you get started on your own social entrepreneurship?

First, find your passion. Or let the passion find you. Another example comes from a friend of ours. Our friend Tammy once bought new computers for her twin boys and their old computers were lying around the house. When their housekeeper saw that the old computers weren't being used and that the boys were using the new ones, she asked Tammy whether she planned to do anything with the old ones because her own son didn't have a computer and any computer would help him with his schoolwork. Tammy was shocked to learn that there were a lot of kids in San Diego without computers.

She gave the housekeeper the unused computers and has since built a very successful non-profit called Computers 2 SD Kids, which collects old computers from hospitals and other big companies that need to update their hardware. The organization now provides computers to kids who normally wouldn't have access to a computer, and these kids are now able to perform better in school and have the same advantages that the kids in higher economic brackets have. Now, the organization has an incredible warehouse and even a full-time driver who goes around and collects old computers. Volunteers wipe out the boards and teach kids how to use the computers. All because somebody asked a question and that person's need struck Tammy.

We always tell our kids to find their passion. We say, "If you're passionate about something, the subject matter will be easy to learn." Likewise, it's easy to start a business when you're passionate about the cause it supports.

Step two is to dive in and learn more about your cause. Go out into the world and go on a trip. Volunteer. There are many volunteer adventures popping up as the new kind of vacation. What if your passion is working with kids in the developing world? On your next vacation, skip the beach resort. Instead, go to a developing country and see whether your passion inspires you to do more. Once you touch and feel your passion, it will become incredibly authentic and real to you. You won't be able to let it go.

When you decide that you want to pair this passion with your entrepreneurial spirit, find a mentor who knows how to start projects well. Or find a family member or a friend—someone willing to give you thoughts and ideas regarding how to begin to develop a framework for a plan or a business of some sort.

And again, don't quit your day job, but kindle that passion and your social entrepreneurial idea. Let it percolate until you and your team are ready from an experience standpoint and you've got the financial standpoint to take that plunge. This might take a month. Or it might take a decade. But as with College Summit, it starts with just four students you tutor. Or as with Computers 2 SD Kids, it starts with just two leftover computers.

When we spoke with a group of young women at Wellesley College, they asked, "Don't you feel overwhelmed? And how did you pick water?"

These young women were so eager and ready to partner in solving some of the world's problems. When we were children, we had the naïve view that we could change the world and solve everything. Then somewhere along the way, we began to learn how large these problems are, how big the world is, how little we are and we began to feel insignificant and disillusioned.

The solution, then, isn't to quit. It's to find a way to impact your own little part of the world. The Torah teaches us that we have an obligation to jump in. Even though we may not finish solving the problem, we have an obligation to start by picking our own little corner of the world to improve. And if we all do our share, then eventually, a ripple effect will occur and the world will feel the healing effects of authentic change.

When we told this to the young lady at Wellesley, we saw relief sweep over her. She just needed to hear someone say, "You know what, being at Wellesley College and being smart and at the top of your class doesn't mean you have the responsibility of solving *all* the world's problems." It's comforting to hear that our passion is toward our small corner of the world.

That student was an immigrant from Africa whose mother died of AIDS. Maybe her issue could be AIDS. Susan G. Komen of the Breast Cancer Foundation had a sister who died of breast cancer. Her passion was personal. And that personal drive fueled an amazing organization. We chose water as our passion because the water walk in Africa spoke to us as a family.

It is contrary to the American spirit to sit out a challenge because it's too big. You don't need to take in the whole world all at once. If you think in terms of small steps and big ideas, nothing is impossible. So what's *your* passion?

CHAPTER 8

The Perfect Storm: Why the Time is Now for Social Entrepreneurship

Where there is passion and desire,
there will always be a new frontier.
– Author Unknown –

WE ALL KNOW THE expression, "Give a man a fish, feed him for a day; teach a man to fish, feed him for a lifetime." Bill Drayton—the social entrepreneur who founded Ashoka, an organization that supports international social entrepreneurship ventures—takes it a step further. He says, "Social entrepreneurs are not content just to give a fish or teach how to fish. *They will not rest until they have revolutionized the fishing industry.*"

Today, the perfect storm is brewing for social entrepreneurs to be able to revolutionize not just the fishing industry but every field. During this time of economic and political turmoil at home and abroad, we have reached a crossroads in the United States and Americans have an important choice to make. We can either rely on the government for help or we can embrace the American entrepreneurial spirit and tackle our problems—and the world's problems—innovatively from the ground up. Now is the ideal time to subscribe to the social entrepreneur calling, and in this chapter, we'll identify the elements of the social entrepreneur's perfect storm.

Before we discuss the "why now," let's first discuss the "who." Once we distinguish social entrepreneurs from traditional entrepreneurs, we will better be able to explain why today's cultural and economic environment is the perfect springboard for the new wave of social entrepreneurs.

A social entrepreneur is one who recognizes a social problem and uses entrepreneurial principles to organize, create and manage a venture to make social change. They are people who "combine the business savvy of Richard Branson with the heart of Mother Teresa." Whether it be in the form of a non-profit or a for-profit entity they are passionate about making money and equally passionate about giving it away. In short, social entrepreneurs want to make a difference *and* a dollar.

Entrepreneurship is a disruption of popular techniques. When Fred Smith started Federal Express, he disrupted the way packages were shipped by offering overnight deliveries. In 1976, when Muhammad Yunus offered microloans to impoverished people in Bangladesh, he did the same thing.

Whereas a traditional entrepreneur such as Fred Smith focuses on generating a profit and a traditional non-profit entrepreneur such as Muhammad Yunus focuses on reaching a social goal, a social entrepreneur generates profit as a means to the social goal. This hybrid model is the one we advocate.

Capitalism not only benefits the person making the buck, but also promotes an environment that creates jobs, increases spending and improves the economy. An organization that seeks to solve a social problem can simultaneously elevate its local community if it employs capitalistic principles.

We've talked about the fact that it would cost just $8 billion to bring clean water and safe sanitation to every human being on earth. That might sound like a daunting number, but we spend more than twice that amount—$15 billion—each year on perfume and $20 billion each year on ice cream. This is not meant to make us feel bad about eating ice cream. Rather we should be aware of the fact that problems such as water are very solvable if we put our hearts and our minds to it. Governments and large non-profit NGOs won't be the ones to solve it as they have had their shot and it hasn't worked out very well. The time is ripe for social entrepreneurs to tackle the issue by being disruptive in their approach. We need people who will be that powerful combination of Fred Smith and Muhammad Yunus.

So who exactly are these people? In other words, what qualities should you possess as a social entrepreneur?

The qualities that make traditional entrepreneurs and the ones that make social entrepreneurs overlap in many ways. This is exciting because if you start down one path and decide you want to experiment with the other, then you will already possess many of the skills you will need in your new endeavor.

First, whether you are a traditional or social entrepreneur, you need a massive work ethic. There's no substitute for hard work. Generally, when people say, "It looks like you're an overnight success; what was your secret?" the answer usually is, "I spent forty years of hard work." But your work ethic must come paired with a second quality—the willingness to drag ideas through the mud. To start something and see it through is a massive undertaking. So unless you have a passion for your endeavors, it will be difficult to sculpt your visions into reality.

A third quality that you must possess as an entrepreneur is the willingness to stay the course even as you receive negative feedback or disappointing results. Any entrepreneurial launch will have moments when the effort looks like it's taking one step forward and two steps back. You are guaranteed starts, stops and plenty of frustrations. The ones who lack resolve will wash out and not persevere. There are, of course, times when letting yourself be washed out is the appropriate business decision. But successful entrepreneurs need the wisdom to know when to endure and how to channel endurance into productivity. You must be able to handle cold water thrown on your idea and figure out how to turn that water into ice cubes. Be proactive with every critique and with every step backwards instead of giving into the temptation to say, "I tried this, it didn't work," and hurrying to the next thing.

Fourth, entrepreneurs must be able to balance creativity with implementation and balance idealism with realism. This is partly why we've been such a great team behind NIKA. While Linda leans more toward creativity and idealism, Jeff possesses more of the implementation and pragmatic realism. Most people are not exactly in the middle. You're naturally a little more right-brained or left-brained, so it's important to find a mentor or a partner who can balance your strengths by providing that other side. All the great ideas in the world are useless without the ability to drag them through the mud to figure out ways to implement them. And conversely, any knowledge of how to implement ideas will be unproductive unless you can think outside the box for that breakthrough idea.

The fifth and final quality that both traditional and social entrepreneurs need is the ability to connect the dots. This means that although you don't know exactly where you're headed, you should work to cover every base to get there. Have a good sense of whom to network with, figure out how to market your product and continue to acquire relevant information so that you can connect all those dots together to create a disruptive and unique business model that will generate profit and also be something you're passionate about.

In addition to those five qualities of entrepreneurs, there are two characteristics that are unique to *social* entrepreneurs. First, social entrepreneurs aren't motivated by profit. Unlike traditional entrepreneurs, social entrepreneurs view profit creation as a means to an end. Solving societal issues or challenges is the impetus for social entrepreneurship, and profit is simply the vehicle to get there.

Secondly, social entrepreneurs must have the ability to infect others with the passion or the cause. Traditional entrepreneurs also need to pass the bug to people they work with, but part of their bark or their selling point is the financial upside. In a social entrepreneurship, the upside isn't the financial benefit; the upside is seeing the societal problem solved. So as a social entrepreneur, you must inspire and educate people so that they develop a strong passion for the cause and become loyal change makers so that they can advocate for your business's social message as well.

Now that we've identified what qualities a social entrepreneur requires, let's dive into the reasons why the current day and age is the ideal setting for a successful social entrepreneurship.

In the 1950s, after World War II, our parents graduated from college and went to work for companies with handshakes that seemingly guaranteed a career with lifelong healthcare benefits and secure pensions. But those golden handshakes disappeared in the 60's with the maturing of the US economy and with increasingly competitive and global markets. Now, we've entered a post-job era in which job security and retirement don't exist for most people. This evolution of the working world has encouraged people to be more entrepreneurial, to work from home and to be more mobile with the help of technology. With this backdrop in mind, we'll touch on five reasons why the time is now ripe for social entrepreneurship.

The first reason is that young people today not only want to make a buck, but also want to contribute to causes larger than themselves. In 2007, UCLA conducted a national poll of college freshmen. Seventy percent of those incoming freshmen—the highest percentage in 36 years—said that they believe it is essential or very important to help others in difficulty. In 2009, a large accounting firm surveyed people between the ages of 18 and 26, and two-thirds of those responders said that they want jobs that permit them to contribute to non-profit groups. Today's young people demonstrate a strong desire to give back to their communities.

Business schools are broadening their approach toward social entrepreneurship aggressively and quickly in order to meet this desire in incoming business students. Thirty business schools, including top-notch universities such as Georgetown, Duke and Harvard, have launched social entrepreneurship programs. The number of law schools that support pro bono programs requiring students to work in a pro bono field for some portion of their schooling has increased by 50% since 2001.

The prevalence of technology may also play a part in stirring up the younger generations' desire to give back. Perhaps because they are so immersed in electronics, they need a means to connect with humanity by becoming involved in social issues. We recently attended a Bat Mitzvah where the girl analyzed this very issue in her Torah portion. Today's kids, youths and even Generation Y's young adults hardly talk on the phone anymore. They text, send instant messages or communicate through their social networking sites. Groups of kids sit around at school and text the other kids they sit next to because they claim that it's easier to text. With that loss of authentic human contact, no wonder today's youths crave a way to plug in to greater social causes. Instead of spending hours on the phone with one person, kids now communicate with 25 to 30 people simultaneously. Their relationships are shallower, but they certainly have better access to people and to information, and they share that information with each other at incredible speeds.

Today's youths have also lost a sense of balance in their high-speed lifestyles. Our son Joshua told us that there are three elements to being a high school student: good grades, an active social life and healthy physical habits such as getting enough sleep. He said that it's impossible to maintain all three, so you have to choose two. Joshua chooses sleep and his social life, and he said that our daughter Nina chooses her social life and good grades, which explains why Nina walks around and looks ready to fall asleep at any moment. A recent high school graduate and close friend of our family's devoted his last two years of high school to his community service and to getting straight A's, but he sacrificed his social life and didn't have very many friends. Parents today don't teach their children how to maintain that healthy life balance because we're also struggling to figure out how to live that way. Jeff says that when he feels he is doing well in at least one of the three important aspects of his life—work, family and exercise—he finds that at least one of the other two is suffering. Oddly, he typically feels the most balanced when he's *not* doing well on all three fronts because that's when he's connecting with all three on equal levels.

Because many of today's parents are always off working, many kids don't have that old-fashioned bond at home with their immediate families. The problem is that these kids are now missing that bond with their friends as well. This may be a reason why the more people become entrenched in their over-programmed lives, the more they gravitate to social issues. They want to feel important. They desire a sense of purpose.

The second reason why the time is ripe for social entrepreneurship is that global issues now greet us front and center through our laptops and smartphones because of the Internet. It's not that these issues didn't exist before; it's that we didn't see them as quickly or as clearly. It is difficult to witness the atrocities of child labor and child soldiers in Darfur in real time and not be moved to become socially engaged in some way. All you have to do is take a quick look at the recent fall of power in Egypt and you will see the profound impact of social media on our society. The impact of Facebook and Twitter is mentioned as one of the core reasons that the change of power occurred.

It wasn't long ago that we were plugging computer lines into phone jacks. Only ten to fifteen years ago, we couldn't use the Internet for much more than email because accessing one page took up too much bandwidth and loading one graphic took hours. Because we can now transfer broadband so easily with nearly no complications, people have access to all the information they could want regarding any current event. We have immediate access to global issues in ways we'd never had, so the reality of these issues also penetrates us in ways it never before could.

Of course, people always spout the variety of pitfalls that come with the Internet—lack of privacy, security risks and the like. If it is mishandled, the Internet *can* be a negative medium for information. But if it is used in positive ways, the Internet can be an incredible resource for today's social entrepreneurs, which brings us to our third point: the Internet is a valuable business partner for social entrepreneurships.

Today, any one of us can be an academic researcher from the living room. We once needed to study the coffee industry in Haiti, and in a period of 4 to 5 days, from our couch, we were able to extract as much information as we needed on the topics of coffee, the coffee industry, Haiti, people to network with, and programs created by the Department of Agriculture—information we never could have had such easy access to before.

Television news has veered from reporting facts to churning opinions, but the large majority of Americans who has access to computers and the Internet can now search any news topic or current event and get twenty-five articles from various political bents. The Internet gives us the freedom to educate ourselves and form our own opinions instead of always being fed one-sided opinions from newscasters.

For those of us who aren't as proactive about seeking out information regarding global issues, we still hear about them from celebrities. A new celebrity trend is to adopt a cause and garner public attention toward that cause, which brings us to reason number four—the coolness factor.

When we were kids, we saw Sally Struthers on cable programs speaking on behalf of ChildFund International. The programs would feature African kids who looked like they were on death's doorstep. Flies would swarm their heads and the entire program was hardly engaging and certainly not "cool." If anything, they were frightening. Programs such as the Peace Corps existed, but they didn't have the same appeal to youths as they do now. Over the last thirty years, with the help of celebrities such as Bono, issues such as poverty alleviation somehow became hip topics in popular culture.

Whether or not you agree with Bono's politics, you have to admit that he's accomplished a tremendous amount for social causes and international aid organizations. Bono takes stadiums crammed with 70,000 kids and fires them up with his music and his philanthropic messages. Musicians such as John Mayer have written songs such as "Waiting on the World to Change" to create awareness, and others have created educational music videos complete with relevant statistics such as Sarah McLachlan's "World on Fire." Of course there are the celebrities who make millions for representing bottled water brands, which is of course their prerogative. However there are celebrities such as Matt Damon and Angelina Jolie who use their platforms and their popularity to create awareness for their global causes.

The fifth and final reason why the time is right for social entrepreneurships is the new access to baby boomer money. Baby boomers who have accumulated significant net worth are now retiring while subscribing to the increasingly popular culture of philanthropy. In 2009, Warren Buffett and

Bill Gates invited 50 to 100 billionaire couples and families to a private dinner, where they challenged them to give away 50% of their net worth over the remainder of their lives to a charitable cause. Almost 50 of them have already agreed to this commitment. The impact that these people alone will have is incredibly significant. Bill Gates, who is giving away $27 billion, for example, is singlehandedly making a huge impact on malaria.

At NIKA, we're donating money to a much smaller degree, but we're not alone. There are plenty of baby boomers like us who don't necessarily have a ton of money, but are giving their time or their resources wherever they can in order to make small dents in the world. These are the seeds of a wave of social entrepreneurships.

All the ingredients are in place to make a significant difference in the world of social entrepreneurships over the next couple decades. Not only do we have the elements of the perfect storm, but we also have a world that's ready to receive and be impacted powerfully by that storm of social entrepreneurships.

First, with baby boomer money and more vehicles available for sustainable funding, benefited NGOs and charities can now transform the way they approach their incomes and their fundraising strategies. Through social entrepreneurships, NGOs and charities can devote more of their resources and time to their causes and to the implementation of creating sustainable businesses within *their* own charities.

Seventy percent of Free the Children's donations come from kids' bake sales, car washes and fundraisers. When a child works hard and hands $50 to Free the Children, the organization has a hard time justifying spending even the smallest percentage of that fundraised money on administrative costs. So in order to allocate all the fundraising money directly to the cause, Free the Children created a for-profit arm called Me to We, which sells paraphernalia, products and accessories to pay for its administrative costs. Social entrepreneurships are now inspiring non-profits such as Free the Children to think innovatively so that they can maximize the use of the money they raise for their causes.

Secondly, social entrepreneurships can help solve the larger societal problems that we haven't been able to tackle over the years. With a number like $8 billion, solving the global water issue is entirely possible, but the current approaches aren't getting the job done. The world is ready to see social entrepreneurships revolutionize the system and disrupt the way we've halfheartedly addressed the global need for clean water.

The third reason our world is ready to embrace social entrepreneurships is that this is a new field that has the ability to marry the creativity and work ethic of today's young people with the excess capital of baby boomers. Social entrepreneurships will give those two different generations a unique opportunity to work together in an entrepreneurial setting for global causes. Fourth, the current generation of young people is already being taught to care about the developing world, and they're being taught in schools to innovate and create. A wave of social entrepreneurships will inspire a powerful boom in innovation. With the creation of entities such as Facebook, young people understand that great fortunes no longer emerge from behind closed doors or in boardrooms or in big cities 1000 miles away. Instead, entrepreneurial ventures can start in dorm rooms and garages, as did brand name companies from Apple to Zappos, from Microsoft to Facebook. There's more computing power in a chip that's used in today's cell phone than there was in the computer that powered the Apollo rocket to the moon. And there's more computing—and connecting—power in an undergraduate's laptop or iPad than in any business office until a decade ago. In the 60s, the chant was, Power To The People. Today, people truly have the power...to accomplish just about anything.

Children are being taught to think the way inventors think. In their science classes, our kids participated in invention fairs, for which they had to create their own inventions. We teach our children to think about products that could revolutionize industries. We encourage them to think about the ways they live life and imagine what they could create to make living better or easier. The right widget or gadget created in the right way could create millionaires overnight.

On October 1, 2010, Peter Thiel, the billionaire founder of PayPal, launched a program that will foster the next generation of tech visionaries by supporting twenty entrepreneurs under the age of 20 with grants of up to $100,000. Thiel stirred up a little controversy by promoting the message that kids don't need to go to college in order to become successful entrepreneurs. But the bottom line is that he understands the creative power of young people and wants to push the next generation to innovate.

Thanks to technology, the world is changing at an exponential rate. But instead of simply wanting to make it to the top and be the masterminds behind that change, today's young people want to make sure that that their global neighbors will also benefit from these changes. This generation of socially minded entrepreneurial youths possesses the exact tools and support it needs to address the developing world's most pressing needs.

Young people want to make a difference and it is important for colleges to adapt their curriculums and their programs to that desire. When our daughter Nina was visiting colleges, the ones that caught her eye were programs that encouraged students to think globally, such as Wharton's Huntsman Program. Today's youths are innovators and entrepreneurs who've got their minds set on international relations and solving problems at the global level. They want to make a buck, but also make a difference.

As the idiom proposes, it is important to be in the right place at the right time. A combination of factors must be in place for an idea or a project to take off and make a sizeable dent in the world. We're writing this book because it is absolutely the right time for social entrepreneurships. The perfect storm is brewing for worldwide change.

With technology, ease of access to capital and youth culture in the favor of social entrepreneurship, there has never been a richer time to become a change maker. For generations, children have been saying, "When I grow up, I want to make the world a better place." Today, we can confidently tell them that as Gandhi once said, they *can* "be the change that they want to see in world." We can even partner with them and begin *now*.

A brief recap of several of the important concepts within this chapter:

Characteristics of Social Entrepreneur

- Passionate about their mission

- Belief in their cause

- Massive work ethic

- Willingness to persevere

- Ability to handle curve balls and adapt

- Ability to balance creativity and implementation

- Ability to connect the dots

Why the Wave of Social Entrepreneurship is Coming

- Young people today want to be a part of something larger than just making money. People in their 40s and 50s are increasingly searching for life meaning

- The Internet is bringing global issues to our laptops 24/7

- The Internet can make any of us academic researchers from our couches

- Celebrities are increasingly using their platforms to promote their causes

- Many of the baby boomers are retiring and donating back a portion of their net worth

CHAPTER 9

The Triple Bottom Line

The time is always right to do what is right.
– Martin Luther King, Jr. –

*T*HE UNITED STATES AVERAGES approximately 30,000 new non-profits each year. These are largely non-profits with little to no sustainable ways to raise money. In this poor economy, even as businesses struggle to survive, these non-profits sprout up all over the country in great numbers with noble intentions, but mostly poor planning. As we talked about in the last chapter, this is absolutely the time for social entrepreneurships. But what exactly does a social entrepreneurship entail? What does the "bottom line" mean for social entrepreneurial businesses? In this chapter, we will answer these questions, introduce you to social entrepreneurship's unique *triple* bottom line and also reveal ten important lessons for the start of your social entrepreneurial venture.

Let's begin with the three main ingredients of a social entrepreneurship. Social entrepreneurships must be **sustainable, entrepreneurial** and **cause-based**. As we mentioned before, ultimately your social entrepreneurship must be able to stand on its own without needing your wallet and without needing fundraising efforts. In addition to financial sustainability, a social entrepreneurship must inherently be entrepreneurial and innovative. Being innovative also means having the ability to be scaled beyond the team that starts it. For example, a local bakery might seem entrepreneurial for a husband and wife team, but it isn't a true entrepreneurial idea unless it can be replicated to reach a broader map of people more quickly and also possesses a unique feature that distinguishes it from other bakeries. Social entrepreneurships ideally bring a systemic change to the status quo of business in their specific arenas. Third, a social entrepreneurship has a humanitarian or social component. It tries to improve society by identifying a problem, challenge or area of opportunity that can be addressed through its efforts.

Now that we've identified the components of a social entrepreneurship, what is its goal—its bottom line? A bottom line refers to the profitability of an organization. In traditional entrepreneurships, this typically means the company's **profits.** How much it can return to its shareholders. Many social entrepreneurships have a double bottom line. They generate profits to maintain the business and also to donate to **the social cause** they support. A triple bottom line adds a third component, which is **the environment.** Organizations with a triple bottom line are concerned with profit, the improvement of a social cause and also minimizing the impact on the environment.

At NIKA, we abide by the triple bottom line. We recently spoke to a company called sOccket, which attempts to do the same. Created by a group of Harvard students who took an engineering class together, sOccket features a soccer ball with an inductive coil embedded inside. Kicking the soccer ball stores energy in the ball so that 15 minutes of kicking results in three hours of LED light. An incredible number of people in the developing world—about 1.5 billion people—have no access to electricity. sOccket seeks to make a difference for these people by providing this small light. In order to create revenue, the company sells these soccer balls in the United States and uses a one-for-one model, where one purchased ball equals one ball donated to the developing world.

TOMS shoes also financially sustains itself through the one-for-one model. For every pair of shoes purchased, TOMS donates a pair to someone without shoes in the developing world. For consumers who want to make a small difference but don't know how, organizations like TOMS, NIKA and sOccket give them an opportunity to become educated on global issues in the developing world while obtaining a consumer good and also giving tangibly to the cause at hand. Americans are good at shopping. The modern, socially conscious American is looking for unique items to buy that can double as a contribution to a good cause, making products like TOMS shoes great double gifts.

The triple bottom line is the ideal goal for a social entrepreneurship, but as we've mentioned throughout this book, all sorts of philanthropic entrepreneurial models exist. When Linda's sister Debbie and our great family friend, Cristina, began their clothing line, Look Within, they chose a different charity to benefit from the proceeds of each trunk show. Debbie donated 10% of her profits from her first trunk show to efforts to aid Sudanese refugees. We're not writing this book to say that every organization should follow the exact NIKA model and give 100% of its profits away. We *are* encouraging you and your entrepreneurship to give within your means or your capacity. Be innovative not just in your business endeavor, but in your giving as well.

Now let's get more practical. We've encountered many well-intentioned people who have the right enthusiasm, but lack the business savvy to implement their social entrepreneurial ideas. In order to impart some of our experiences with people who want to get their feet wet in social entrepreneurships but aren't quite sure how, we've compiled a list of ten lessons to keep in mind while creating your startup.

1. **Begin with the end in mind.** Borrowed from Stephen Covey's *The Seven Habits of Highly Effective People*, the first lesson to starting your social entrepreneurship is to think about your final destination even during phase one. Ask yourself what success looks like when you get there. Whenever Jeff buys a company, he writes the selling memorandum for that company right away. He writes it to create sizzle or interest for a prospective future buyer in order to figure out where the holes are.

Then he spends the next 2 to 3 years working on those holes to meet the standard of that selling memorandum. Keeping the end in mind often gives the present a productive perspective.

2. **Be transparent with your donations.** Even if you can't donate large sums of money, start donating early and make these donations public. This will help present your business and market it to your community so that you have credibility when your business takes off. It's easy to claim to donate 100% of your business's profits when you first begin because you haven't had any profits yet. But if you make known your track record of charitable giving, then people will see that you're serious about your causes. In this spirit, at NIKA, we took a leadership stance on making donations. On our NIKA website, we have a page that lists the organizations that have received donations from us. We include the charities' contact information, what the donations involve, the actual amount, and the status regarding whether it has been committed or actually donated. sOccket, likewise, tracks the number of soccer balls they've donated and how many people they've brought light to on their website. This kind of transparency adds authenticity to the business.

3. **Act boldly but honestly with your financial backing.** You might be one of the most humble people on the planet. But when you talk about your financial backing, present your company the way you would present yourself when applying to a college. You certainly don't want to lie or misrepresent the truth, but be sure to put your best foot forward. Potential investors, vendors, consumers and charities all want to know whom you're financially associated with so that they can be assured that you're legitimate.

4. **Find like-minded people to embrace the brand.** We've been lucky at NIKA to have found dozens of people who love the concept, love the product and love the idea. Once your business and your message can infect people enough so that they also run with the ball, then you've hit the jackpot. Right now, NIKA is having a bit of difficulty in Boston with our sell-through and with getting new merchants on board. We've kicked around some ideas as it makes sense to retrench and pull back in order to defend our West Coast base instead. But when we spoke with Kara who has been with us from the beginning, she was really disappointed. She assured us that there's enthusiasm for NIKA in Boston and told us to push through. Finding people who embrace your vision and reinforce your brand is priceless. These are the people who give you leverage and who, on some days, push even stronger than you do.

5. **Your brand has to have a strong value proposition.** The price and quality of your product must make sense not only for the consumer, but also for the distribution channel. Although someone in your distribution channel might be an advocate of your social cause, he or she will sign on to your product only if it makes sense financially. At the end of the day, the purchasing manager of the local distributor will be evaluated based on the profit margin and the turns he gets on the product. So even though his boss might like NIKA and want it to work, the person in the trenches will be the one who judges the product based on numbers.

     When you present a new product, you need to offer a good value proposition. People aren't going to pay $20 for a bottle of water. On the same token, people aren't going to buy the water at any price if it tastes awful. Typically, the retail price of a product is four to five times its manufactured cost. For example, our cost to make a bottle of water is roughly a quarter. But once that bottle is sold through the distribution channel and you tack on freight costs and various distribution costs, the bottle sells for roughly a dollar. Remember that whatever your cost, you'll have to multiply it by 4 or 5 times simply to get it to the market. Also be sure to check for quality. If the sOccket soccer ball doesn't kick like a normal soccer ball, then the company might have a great idea, but it won't take. Or if that ball is five times the price of an average soccer ball, the business won't be sustainable. This is one of the reasons that we say in the beginning your social business must be three parts business and one part social giving. This might not be the most creative part of starting your social entrepreneurship, but it is definitely one of the most essential.

6.   **Outsource as much as possible.** Newman's Own generates about $30 million a year in profits, yet it employs only about 35 to 40 direct employees because it outsources the manufacturing of its salad dressings, soups and other products. The company makes its cost variable by going to co-packers and contract manufacturers. NIKA aims to do the same. We outsource all of the bottling, co-packing, label making and website development. You might pay a little more for this on a variable basis, but the point is that it's variable. We know of another bottled water company that made a grave and potentially fatal mistake. The company had a strong brand name and was growing nicely. However they decided to build their own manufacturing for their bottling. Their cost to make a case of water on a full cost basis ended up being 3 x what they could have spent outsourcing the manufacturing and keeping it variable.

Keep your *fixed* costs—your head count, offices, et cetera—at a low number.

7. **Try to learn tough business lessons on someone else's nickel first.** If you can, gain experience working in another startup environment where you can wear many different hats. The skills and knowledge you acquire will be invaluable when you're suddenly doing it on your own. Invariably, you will make mistakes in any entrepreneurial setting. But it's always better to learn on someone else's nickel when possible. Of course, this doesn't mean that you want to screw up on someone else's payroll. It also doesn't mean that you have to put your ideas on hold. If you have the opportunity to gain relevant startup experience, take that opportunity, and in the meantime, nurture your ideas the way you would a hobby. Instead of playing an extra round of golf, spend a little extra time on your business idea. Then when the timing is right and you're ready to step off the high board, you'll even be able to do it blindfolded.

8. **Push through the moments when quitting seems logical.** Oftentimes, the difference between success sand failure is razor thin. When you begin a startup, nearly every other week, you'll find yourself asking, "Are we doing the right things? Do we really want to write another check when we've been hit hard by the recession? Will this come to anything?" So how do you know when to stick it out versus when to throw your hands up and quit? Study the market trends related to your services or your product and consider your competitors. Assess how those competitors will affect your business. Then weigh your risks, your position in the marketplace and weigh whether you'll have to sell everything you own to keep going—and whether

you'll want to. If in your gut, it makes sense to readjust your whole lifestyle, redo everything and keep going with your eyes wide open, go for it. Then if you do that and fail, the plug will be pulled automatically, but at least you went in with your eyes open. Also, make sure that you have your family's support should you be unsuccessful. Determine whether you and your family are prepared to adjust your lifestyle if the endeavor doesn't pan out.

Having a couple independent advisors—people you have confidence in—to serve as a board of consultants is a good idea. Be sure to line up a variety of people. Appointing three people who come from accounting backgrounds won't be useful because they'll all approach your business from a critical perspective and be less aggressive about rolling the dice. You should keep one of those accounting or finance people and then have at least one person who understands the market side or the cause side of your business. Use these people to test the water when you're tempted to pull the plug. But remember that if you *do* choose to quit, it's very difficult to regain momentum for that entrepreneurship. One of the factors that influenced us to be entrepreneurial was a television program that interviewed eight senior citizens and aired at two in the morning. When asked about their regrets, all eight said that they wished that they had taken more risks in their professional careers. Set a high bar for quitting. Sometimes, the cost of giving up is greater than the cost of staying put.

9. **Find a mentor or a partner who balances you.** We've touched on this in previous chapters, and it's important enough to mention again. If you're an idea person, partner with somebody who is an implementer. If you're a great accountant but not really sales-oriented, partner with someone whose marketing

background matches your financial background. Too many startups blow their fuse because they lack a system of checks and balances. Partners with different strengths can be great sources of constructive criticism or tangible support with regard to new ideas.

10. **Remember that everything takes** *twice* **as long with** *twice* **as much money.** All startups follow this *Rule of Two*. It is rare to find a startup that comes in on time and on budget. By nature, humans are optimists. We tend to overestimate what we are capable of and then become discouraged when we realize how off our calculations were. If you remember this final lesson, starting your social entrepreneurship and following through will be much more encouraging and much less disheartening.

When we shared these ten lessons at Harvard recently, the students gave us positive feedback. In light of *The Social Network* and Mark Zuckerberg's story, young people are craving that energizing entrepreneurial environment where you come up with the next new big idea and work 15-hour days to see it through to fruition. Along with the young people who are attaching themselves to this movement, middle-aged people are also using social entrepreneurships as a platform to relieve the modern day midlife crisis. There is a new spirit in Americans and in other parts of the world to want to transition from success to significance. People in their forties and fifties want to know that their lives made a difference in somebody's life, and an illicit affair or a new Corvette won't give them that satisfaction.

People everywhere are itching to make a difference, and we hope that the NIKA story can be a catalyst of motivation for some of those people. If you have an entrepreneurial idea, let it percolate. Mull over it even if you do it over the larger course of your life. You don't want to be hit by a brick wall at fifty and be caught flatfooted with the realization that you're not being fulfilled by your life choices or by your career. Whether you're thinking about a social entrepreneurship at 25 years old or you've just come upon this at age 45, find your passion. Then develop that passion into something meaningful with positive social implications. Educate yourself and look for a problem that hasn't been solved. Then as you develop that passion and the idea matures, find a partner who can back you financially. Or if your own financial situation has changed, make an investment to see your project through.

If starting a social entrepreneurship from scratch is daunting, but you desire to be a part of this movement, brainstorm creatively to figure out ways you can contribute to startups that already exist. Perhaps you could moonlight with a non-profit and help it create a sustainability function within its business. Or you could explore the idea of a Chief Sustainability Officer, who generally exists in the environmental arena, but whose role and function can be translated into the social realm.

If you're better able to give financially than to give of your time, websites such as www.charitynavigator.org can help you research and rate charities. The Internet is a phenomenal resource. At NIKA, we prefer to physically go to touch and feel the projects we give back to, which helps us maintain a solid understanding of the people who lead these organizations. Craig and Marc Kielburger with Free the Children will come to our house or we'll go to their events or to their projects in the developing world. Same with George Guimaraes of Project Concern International. Project Concern and NIKA have even done joint events in the United States. Not everybody has the luxury to visit the charities they give to firsthand, but with websites and video blogs, it's become much easier to keep track of and follow the organizations and causes you support.

Raising a business is like raising a child. You birth the idea and see it through its infancy until it matures into a booming entity. When we began our first business as a startup, we used that analogy quite a bit. When you watch your business evolve and grow, you find yourself making decisions the way a parent does. You don't always get it right, but you base your decisions on good, wise foundations that are, hopefully, not too influenced by your emotional attachment. When you raise a small child, you think about what's best for that child. While you certainly can't compare the love of a child to that of a business, applying that same philosophy to starting your own business can help you get off on the right foot.

We've written this portion of the book to give you practical tools to think about the ways you can affect the world. But in addition to those tools, we want to impart encouragement. If you feel the wheels turning and ideas brewing in your mind, take your blinders off. It's okay to take risks—even in this economy. The more educated and analytical we become, the more facts we accumulate and the more we begin to oversimplify these facts. For example, ninety percent of all businesses fail. The temptation is to internalize this detail and then over-intellectualize the process and all the things that could go wrong with a startup.

When we fixate on the rules we should follow—including everything we've laid out in this chapter—we are in danger of forgetting the larger-than-life stories of the Richard Bransons and the Donald Trumps. We dismiss the Ted Turners who take the gunslinger entrepreneur approach because they don't know enough *not* to do it. These stories show us that there are merits to assessing risks, but also merits to ignoring them. On the same token, we don't have to be gun slinging, incredible personalities to be entrepreneurs. We can sit in our bedrooms to strategize and dream.

To recap the ten lessons learned in doing a social entrepreneurial start up:

1. **Begin with the end in mind—visualize what success looks like in 3-5 years**

2. **Be transparent with your donations**

3. **Act boldly but honestly with your financial backing**

4. **Find like-minded people to embrace the brand**

5. **Price the value proposition well**

6. Outsource as much as possible

7. Try to learn tough business lessons on someone else's nickel first

8. Push through the moments when quitting seems logical

9. Find a mentor or a partner who balances you

10. Remember that everything takes twice as long with twice as much money

In this chapter, we've outlined ten lessons to guide you as you begin your social entrepreneurial venture with its possible triple bottom line. The 90% of businesses that fail are the ones that still have several of these lessons to learn. Now, it's time for you to implement those lessons and turn them into a business plan fit for that other ten percent.

CHAPTER 10

The Ripple Effect: Leadership for Social Entrepreneurs

If your actions inspire others to dream more,
learn more, do more and become more, you are a leader.
– John Quincy Adams –

*N*ow let's shift our focus from your social entrepreneurship to you—the visionary and leader behind your venture. You might cringe when you hear the word "leader" because maybe you—like many people—have bought into the notion that you don't have the right qualifications to be a leader. But we've observed over the years that the amount of experience you have in leadership positions gives little indication of whether or not you can be a successful leader. The ticket to becoming a great leader begins with something simple: *passion*. Whether you've already managed dozens of people or are just now brainstorming business ideas from your dorm room, this chapter is for you. In this chapter, we'll discuss The Ripple Effect, the NIKA guide to leadership for social entrepreneurs.

Before we begin, let's look at Linda's story. It's hard to believe now that Linda was so shy growing up that by the time she graduated high school, she couldn't even muster the courage to call 4-1-1 to talk to the operator. Most people might assume that a teenager who can't even talk to strangers on the phone has no future leading boardroom presentations, but Linda's brother-in-law, Al, thought differently. Al was an attorney who noticed how painfully shy Linda was so he decided to hire her as his receptionist in his law office. Through that opportunity, Linda slowly conquered her fear of talking to strangers. Linda's willingness to test her limits through this experience was the starting point for her future as a businesswoman and successful employer. Just because you've never considered yourself a leader doesn't mean that you can't be one now.

When Linda was growing up, she didn't fit the profile of a typical outgoing leader, but thanks to her Jewish upbringing, she was passionate about the world and serious about justice. A **passion** for your cause, paired with **self-control**, is all the magic you need in order to start becoming the ideal leader for your social entrepreneurship. A pebble dropped in a body of water creates ripples, or a sequence of rings beginning with the largest concentric circle. In The Ripple Effect, the pebble is your passion and self-control. That pebble creates what will be the largest ripple, which are the basics you need in order to get in the game: **intelligence, experience, motivation** and **integrity.** The next largest ripple consists of **adaptability, listening skills** and **your risk profile,** while the smallest and tightest circle represents your **strategy, vision** and **action.** Sharpening your basic qualities in the largest ripple is crucial because you're always only as good as the last ripple. The next ripple won't exist or be as large as it can be unless the last one is there.

The fundamentals that fuel leadership are *passion* and *self-control*—the makeup of your pebble. One quote we've always loved is, "There are many things in life that will capture your eye, but few will capture your heart. These are the ones to pursue. These are the ones worth keeping." But in addition to the passion that captures the heart, a good leader also needs to begin with the head. A major reason that 90% of businesses fail is that they launch off of great ideas, but aren't steered with enough self-control. Most people tend to lean in one direction or the other, but they're not right in the middle. As we've mentioned earlier in the book, this is why it's important to have a mentor or a partner who can balance you in either direction. Business is full of different push/pulls. You need one foot on the accelerator and another foot on the brake. If you're right brained, you need someone left brained. If you're creative, you need someone logical.

Finding the right passion is just as important as finding the right partner. Your day job could be the source of your passion, but oftentimes, that's not the case. In order to find your passion, try dozens of experiments. When we first started dating, we were interested in the Special Olympics, so we volunteered for a snow skiing weekend in New Jersey for a Special Olympics Day. We enjoyed it, but the experience didn't click in terms of passion—not withstanding the fact that the person Jeff helped during the day didn't really want to be there. We volunteered and became involved with dozens of different efforts over the years before we discovered our passion for water.

The beauty of the United States is that we're all individuals and each of us is one of many—*e pluribus Unum.* Jeff recently had breakfast with a surgeon whose passion is fixing cleft palates. Countries like the Ukraine kill babies born with this defect, so the doctor adopted the cause in order to fix the smiles of children and give them a chance at life. Maybe you're not a doctor. Maybe playing tennis is your passion. Then use your niche in tennis to start a fundraiser or an activity that marries your love of tennis with a greater purpose. Open as many doors as you need to in order to find the right passion that resonates with you.

Your passion gives you the ability to inspire others. Inspiration is a key to leadership because it instills your passion in the other people deciding to join your cause. Inspiration also comes from a worldview founded in gratitude. It's important to feel grateful to be alive and to be able to wake up every morning. We're grateful to have a beautiful home with beautiful children in a beautiful country full of opportunities. But even without all of that, we practice being thankful for what we have whether we have a lot or we have a little. If you approach life with this attitude, then you'll always have enough inspiration to influence others positively.

Once you have the right combination of passion and self-control, you've begun The Ripple Effect. The first and largest ripple your pebble makes are your four basics of leadership: *intelligence, experiences, motivation* and *integrity.* These building blocks will get you in the arena so that you can play the game, but they won't win the game for you.

While cognitive intelligence is an important quality for a leader, people who are generally on the higher end of the intelligence bell curve sometimes suffer from a disadvantage. We've found that people who are cognitively intelligent sometimes rely on that skill set so much that they don't develop the other skills they need. This mentality is similar in a high school athlete who is successful and plans to go on to become a professional athlete. If that student has relied on his athletic prowess and hasn't developed any other skill sets, but tears his ACL or gets into an accident, then he has nothing to fall back on and nowhere to go. Cognitive intelligence is similar in that it can get you very far and it can get you there very fast. But at the end of the day, unless you can balance that intelligence with other skill sets, you won't be an effective leader. You can be a genius, but this won't help you move forward if you can't talk your way out of a paper bag or if other people don't want to follow you.

Conversely, if you're lacking in an area such as cognitive intelligence, surround yourself with people whose strengths can offset your weaknesses. Jeff's father is an example of someone who was average in intelligence, but not insecure about it. He was confident enough to surround himself with talented, smart people who made him look good. Many people are threatened by others who possess attributes that they don't have, so they don't hire the people who could potentially bolster their business. We're not all good at the same things, and that's the beauty of humankind. The first big rule to parenting is never to compare your kids to each other. We teach our kids not to compare themselves, but to celebrate the uniqueness of each individual. If you apply this in your organization, you'll be better able to create a team environment in which you celebrate the value of each person.

It's also important to remember the difference between intelligence and wisdom. Linda's grandmother, who married at age 13 and gave birth to twelve children, was illiterate. At her funeral, thousands of people from her community showed up because although she couldn't read a word, her mother, who also couldn't read or write, had passed down to her the wisdom of the Torah. All kinds of people would approach Linda's grandmother with their problems because she possessed genuine, simple wisdom. When our kids struggle with their grades, we always remind them that Hitler was a straight-A student with a high IQ. What *really* matters to us is what kind of people our kids are becoming and what kind of character they have. As parents, we emphasize the importance of being kind, being good and being regular contributors to society. Cognitive intelligence is great, and attaining wisdom only makes that gift that much stronger.

Linda often struggles because she didn't have the privilege of a college education. She entered the workforce right after high school and she sometimes deals with the insecurity of wondering whether she knows how to write a proper essay or is able to do the research that her kids can do in as short an amount of time. But she feels confident in her gifts of wisdom because she has always gone out of her way to be a student of life. Linda loves learning, and although she didn't have a formal education, she tries to advance her knowledge in the areas that she's passionate about.

Experience is also one of the greatest teachers for leaders. The experiences that shape our ability to lead begin at a very young age. Jeff's first memorable leadership experience was the process of applying for his lifeguard certification at age 15. Although he studied for the certification, he hadn't studied nearly as much as he should have because he not only failed dismally on the water test, but also failed even more dismally on the written test. Jeff was really cut up about this for a long time and continued to look back at the failure as a negative event. But in his late 20s, Jeff finally realized that this bad experience actually taught him to be a leader who never takes on anything without being completely prepared.

Of the six meaningful business experiences that Jeff has had, four of them have been successful, but the two unsuccessful ones are the ones that have taught him the most from a leadership standpoint. A losing experience gives you a better paradigm for seeing what works or what doesn't work. In the most difficult situations, you discover what you're really made of. As the saying goes, what doesn't kill you only makes you stronger. It's important to hold on to your experiences—both good and bad—as a foundation for leadership in order to practice learning from your mistakes. One good friend of ours was involved in several businesses, but each endeavor blew up in a blaze of glory because this friend wasn't able to learn from his experiences and had a habit of repeating his mistakes.

Motivation is also an important foundation for leadership. We've all heard of the athlete who is the first to show up on the football field and the last to leave it. Or the basketball player who shoots free throws for six hours a day. A leader must have a similar drive. We once heard that the secret to a successful 40-hour workweek is to work 60 hours. There's no substitute for hard work. People often want to reap the benefits of success without putting in the time. But having that strong work ethic comes from being motivated. If you're motivated and intellectually curious about something, you'll work hard and search for opportunities to better yourself.

Integrity is the final aspect of the largest ring in The Ripple Effect. Someone once said, "The highest courage is to dare to be yourself in the face of adversity. Choosing right over wrong, ethics over convenience, and truth over popularity … these are the choices that measure your life. Travel the path of integrity without looking back for there is never a wrong time to do the right thing." Kids today don't learn that there are a set of truths and principles. They're taught that everything is relative and that even morally wrong decisions can be justified. But there is no relativism when it comes to human decency. A Holocaust survivor and famous psychologist Viktor Frankl said in his book, *Man's Search for Meaning,* "there are only two races in the human race, the decent and the indecent."

Integrity is important because leaders must lead by example. Leaders should never do something that they wouldn't want their employees to do. When Linda was pregnant with Nina, she asked Jeff's mother, who had her PhD in child Development, what single most important piece of advice she would give to new parents. Jeff's mother said that kids always do what you do. They never do what you tell them to do. If you tell your child not to lie, but they see you lying and lying, your child will learn to lie. Leadership is about modeling integrity for the people you lead.

The next circle in The Ripple Effect highlights a leader's *adaptability, listening skills* and *risk profile.* First, the ability to adapt yourself to different situations is a key component to leadership. We all know certain people who can't mesh well with certain other people, and you have to take into account their inability to get along when you invite them to an event. Then there are others who get along with everybody seamlessly. Leaders need to practice the skills of adaptability to be able to get along in every situation with all kinds of people. Leaders have to be able to go out on the shop floor to interact with the machine operator and ask him about his kids and his family. The most successful leaders understand the various facets of their employees that are impacting them at work and at home. Leaders also need to be able to make effective boardroom-level presentations. If you can make a great board presentation, but people shudder when you walk down the shop floor, then you won't be able to break down certain barriers of communication, and your employees won't be able to reveal their true selves. Breaking these walls is crucial in a good business because only when you hear what people are really thinking are you able to understand what needs to happen to exact change effectively.

We once bought a successful company of about 400 employees. Everybody was nervous about us coming in and screwing up the company because they didn't understand us well enough to know that we wouldn't come in and fix things that weren't broken. So we created something called "Principles to Preserve and Opportunities for Change." We gave each employee a sheet of paper that asked what principles they most wanted to preserve in the business and what opportunities they saw for change. The themes were very consistent. The company had been very successful so it had an attractive bonus program, which was the number one principle to preserve. That was an easy one, which we weren't going to monkey with anyway. But there were great opportunities for change that people identified as well. Because we were able to adapt to the situation and communicate effectively with the employees, we were able to improve an already thriving business.

This method of leadership—participative management—empowers the employees in the business. At NIKA, we use participative management to get everyone brainstorming about everything from the name of the company to the pictures we use on the labels. This encourages everyone to take on more active roles in the creation of the business and also gives you access to a larger pool of ideas. But it's important not to mistake participative management for a democracy. In business, one person will always have to make the decision. If you have too many people making decisions, you become a management by committee, which hardly ever gets things done. Sometimes, you'll want to delegate the decision-making responsibility to another responsible individual, but you'll have to adapt to that person's process, which might be different from yours.

Management team diversity is also an important component for coming up with the right strategy and vision for your entrepreneurship. "Diversity" doesn't refer to ethnic diversity as much as it refers to people with different perspectives. We all approach situations through the paradigms of our experiences and the environments we were raised in. If you have a group of people who are of the same backgrounds, then you may all get along very well, but you won't necessarily get that diversity of thought. Challenge the default ways you deal with problems. Instead of trying to fit your square peg into a round hole, practice being adaptable to each situation and to each employee's needs.

When Linda managed the cellular phone business that she and her brother and sister started, she had two challenges. She was a woman leading a group of men, and she was a layman leading a group of skilled technicians and mechanics. In order to earn the respect of her employees, Linda had to adapt to their knowledge and expertise. She didn't know where the harness of a cell phone needed to be installed in a Jaguar versus a BMW, but she knew enough to know that there was a difference. So Linda hired the right technician to oversee the other twenty technicians that were doing more installations than she was. She learned the ropes quickly, empowered her technicians to make the decisions they were better equipped to make, and adapted herself in order to make sure that their business was the best installation facility for high-end vehicles in the community. Because she pushed herself in this way, her technicians trusted her and were willing to follow her and her vision even when they knew more than she did in the technical realm.

Talented people don't want to be micromanaged. They want the freedom to make their own decisions. They might make a wrong decision here or there, but so might the boss. It's important to create an environment where every employee feels that his or her voice is heard. This is especially important in social entrepreneurial businesses because typically, you'll be paying the people you work with very little or no money. The people working in your organization are there because they're inspired by the cause and passionate about your efforts. If you micromanage them and insist that every little thing comes back to you for approval, then they won't want to stick around to work with you, especially if they're doing this as volunteers.

Wendy, one of the young ladies who used to work for us, left us after seven years of hard work in order to start a family. When we reconnected years later, she said that working for us was the most fun and the most empowered she'd ever felt in a workplace. When everyone works toward the same goal, it feels like family. We try to create an atmosphere where people aren't afraid to take risks and make wrong decisions. We understand that wrong decisions are part of the journey. When people see that it's okay to make mistakes, they're more apt to put their whole heart into the organization.

Leaders also need to sharpen their listening skills. We always tell our kids the old saying that God gave us one mouth and two ears, which should be a sign that we should listen twice as much as we talk. Jeff always listens to people thoroughly. When he listens, Jeff never reacts until he fully hears what was said and then also regurgitates it back to make sure that he heard correctly. Some people talk so much that you can have an entire conversation with them, learn everything about them and at the end of the conversation, find that that person has learned nothing about you.

You need to listen as a leader because you don't want to miss that one nugget of information that might contradict everything that the person just told you, which may tell you that this person is untrustworthy. Or you may hear one common thing over and over again, which validates what the person has communicated. We try to break bread with a prospective employee and his or her spouse because it is in those moments when you're passing the butter and making casual comments that you really learn whether that person is someone you want to be tied to.

Leadership also requires a certain appetite for risk. A quote we've adopted is "Courage is daring to take that first step, or a different path. It is the decision to place your dreams above your fears." Linda came from a very risk-tolerant background, which is fairly common for people who come from relatively poor environments. Jeff came from an upper-middle-class background so he was raised with more of a push-pull between being risk-tolerant and risk-averse. But both of us were more afraid of mediocrity than we were of failure. So we took risks. We know that if we fail, we'll simply pick up the pieces and move forward.

The next and final ripple consists of *strategy, vision* and *action*. A leader with a sharp strategy and vision needs to be one who can take in hundreds of inputs, critiques and comments. A leader must also be able to filter out the good from the bad because some of the input might be essential, but most of them will be useless red herrings. Discernment is a key component for coming up with the right strategy or vision for your social entrepreneurship, meaning, you have to make sure you're climbing the right tree in the right forest. If you climb the right tree but in the wrong forest, you'll find yourself sitting up at the top above all the other trees in your forest, but you'll be looking over at the forest that you want to be in. If you climb the wrong tree in the right forest, you might get to the top of the tree but find that although you're in the right forest, there are still hundreds of other trees that are much taller than yours.

Another leadership quality that we have ascribed to is the ability to assess and act. People who do extraordinary things are usually people who have a "bias for action." These are the people who make decisions without hesitation. They aren't paralyzed by analysis or fear, and they understand that even the wrong decision implemented well can turn out okay. But if you just sit there and don't make any decision at all, you could be at a disadvantage. As the CEO of a company, Jeff tends to make approximately 25 decisions a day, and they're not all going to be right. He aims to make sure that on average, 80% of those decisions are right. And if he can catch what's wrong with the other 20% and manage their risks, then he's winning the game. As a leader, you have to be able to assess when it is better to do something than to do nothing.

Practice taking risks. If this is difficult for you, then as we've mentioned before, try to learn on someone else's nickel first. If you're sitting in a huge corporation and unhappy pushing pencils around every day, then try out a smaller business where you can be an employee who practices a more varied skill set and makes more important decisions. Wherever you are, it's also important to study the boss or the owner. Jeff has learned more from the bosses that he didn't like than from the bosses that he liked because he generally agrees with the approach and concepts of the bosses he liked. If you observe a leader you dislike, you'll quickly get an understanding of the kind of management style that you don't want to have. Jeff once worked for a person who treated people very poorly. When he walked into a room, everybody scurried. He possessed degrees from the best schools, but didn't understand how to treat people as people and not as chess pieces. When he came into the company, he didn't care whether an employee had accomplished superb work there for a number of years. If he didn't find a use for someone immediately, then he got rid of that person.

That was the boss that taught us about the importance of decentralization in decision-making. Because this individual had a technical background, he had the need to be right a high percentage of the time. In his prior field one needed to be thorough and to be right—almost to a fault. But this boss transferred this value to our business and had a hard time trusting others. He wanted to centralize the decision making so much that he eventually ended up making most of the company's decisions himself instead of letting them be made out in the field. The concept of centralization can make a lot of sense because from an efficiency standpoint, you're dealing with fewer overheads. But as we observed this individual, we saw that the more he centralized, the less he could do. He basically became the bottleneck in the decision making process.

If you have to be right 100% of the time, you can't be productive. Instead of making the 20 to 25 decisions you need to make, you end up making four or five because you're caught up in making sure they're right. Then when those 15 to 20 other decisions aren't being made, you constipate the system. And when you constipate the system, nothing gets done, people get frustrated and the business comes to a screeching halt. Decentralization involves pushing relevant decision making down to the lowest possible level in an organization. Aside from the five to ten percent of people who are on either tail of the bell curve of intelligence, we are all, for the most part, of fairly comparable cognitive intelligence. Therefore, the guy running the machine on the shop floor is probably equally as smart in his field and as capable as the CEO of the company. That person on the shop floor is also closer to knowing and understanding the issues in his department, so he will most likely make better decisions than the CEO could.

Leadership boils down to empowering the people around you. As a leader, your goal is to encourage everyone to buy into your vision and into what you're trying to accomplish. When you make everyone around you feel empowered and like a crucial part of the team, then you can come up with a more comprehensive strategy to run the most successful entrepreneurial venture possible. To use an example from the traditional business world, on Friday afternoon at 5PM, what's going to inspire your employee to want to make that last sales call? You will never know whether or not he makes that sales call, so in order for him to take the initiative to make that last call, he needs to feel empowered and self-motivated.

All of these leadership qualities in The Ripple Effect are connected and interrelated. You need the larger ripples in order for the smaller ones to exist, but if the smaller ripples are strong, they also push out the large ripples and make them even larger. In the same way, we're all connected to each other. The essence of leadership is taking care of each other and being a good steward of the people who work for us. Linda just read a book by Nathan Laufer called *The Genesis of Leadership*. This book uses the Bible to teach us about vision, values and leading change. Leadership always comes back to one question: Are we our brothers' keepers? The people you lead and take care of are the backbone of your organization. They are the ones who will carry your vision to fruition. The future success of your social entrepreneurship begins with you and your relationship with those people who work for you.

We'd like to summarize "the Ripple Effect"—NIKA's guide to leadership. It's concentric circles created by the dropping of a pebble or catalyst into the water:

The largest ripple, or the foundation, consists of the building blocks to leadership:
- Intelligence
- Experiences and the ability to learn from them
- Motivation, work ethic and energy
- Trust and integrity

The next circle is the Personal Emotions:
- Adaptability
- Listening, intuition and empathy
- Risk

Specific to your situation:
- Strategy and vision
- The ability to assess and act

And the difference maker is the catalyst or the pebble:
- Passion with self-control

Part Three

Your Story

We cannot always build the future for our youth,
but we can build our youth for the future.

– Franklin D. Roosevelt –

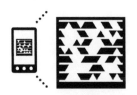

Get the free mobile app at
http://gettag.mobi

CHAPTER 11

What Problem is Calling You?

Big dreams create the magic that stir men's souls to greatness.
– Bill McCartney –

*W*E INTRODUCED YOU TO the NIKA story in part one of this book and we defined social entrepreneurship in part two. Now that you're aware of the skill sets and mindsets required for social entrepreneurships, let's move forward to part three—*your* story.

Just like William Jennings Bryan's quote *"Destiny is not a matter of chance. It's a matter of choice. It's not a thing to be waited for. It's a thing to be achieved."* If an opportunity knocks at your door, don't invite it in and sit down to dine with it. Grab the opportunity by the throat, wrestle it to the ground and take advantage of it right then and there. But before you can seize an opportunity, you have to open the door. And before you open the door, you have to know what an opportunity sounds like when it knocks. This chapter will talk about how to discern which opportunities are calling you.

As you think about your own social entrepreneurial story, brainstorm what problem or cause will fuel your efforts. Some people seek and find the problem that they want to solve, but other times, problems find people. When problems find you, you have a choice. You can dwell in the pain of your misfortune or you can do something about it. Race for the Cure's Nancy Goodman is a good example of someone who took advantage of the problem that found her. She didn't wake up one morning and say, "I'm going to create the largest breast cancer awareness program in the world." Nancy made a promise to her sister that she would work to end breast cancer. Nancy was affected by her sister's breast cancer-related death so she used her emotions and passion for a greater purpose.

At last year's Yom Kippur service, we heard Daniel Pearl's father, Judea Pearl, speak. Daniel Pearl was a reporter for *The Wall Street Journal,* and he was kidnapped and killed by Al-Qaeda in 2002. Daniel's father said that his family could have sat back and mourned Daniel's death without doing anything about it, but instead, they used it as an opportunity to create the Daniel Pearl Foundation in order to help others. His determination not to settle in the pain but rise above it is truly incredible.

There are plenty of examples of people who have turned their misfortunes into blessings that could help others. General Doron Almog of the Israel Defense Forces had a son born with autism so severe that he never spoke a word. The general travels and speaks on behalf of his son's autism and on behalf of Aleh Negev, a world class facility that provides services to people with severe handicaps in southern Israel.

John Walsh, the man who created the television program, *America's Most Wanted,* is a father whose son was murdered by a serial killer in 1981. Instead of choosing to be a father who walks away from the issue and spends his life being bitter about what happened, John chose to do everything possible to help all missing kids. His program even led detectives to Elizabeth Smart's abductors in 2002.

Social entrepreneurs are people who possess a global perspective. When tragedy strikes, they understand that there are others who've suffered from that same tragedy, so their empathy for those others evolves into a passion, which becomes an idea and an organization. If a problem has found you, you can serve as a powerful source of inspiration to others dealing with a similar pain. You can be a leader even in your grief. Dr. Ken Druck is a great example of someone who possesses the sensitivity to speak compassionately to parents who have lost a child because he has lost a daughter. It is difficult to understand someone in the trenches unless you've been there, too. Harness your misfortunes so that you can inspire others to do something about their problems as well.

Of course, a tragic experience is not a requirement for launching your social entrepreneurship. Most people have to hunt for the problem they want to solve. In order to figure out what problem might be calling you, identify your passion. In order to identify your passion, put yourself out into the world and get involved. Trial and error is a natural part of this process. We mentioned in the last chapter that we tried to get involved with a Special Olympics group but found that this particular cause, while an incredible cause and extraordinarily important, didn't connect with us at the highest level. We volunteered at a variety of different organizations before we found the water issue. The more you search and the more different things you try, the easier it becomes to narrow in on the cause you will adopt.

So how do you even begin finding an organization to try out? First, turn off the television and get off your couch! We tell our kids that TV is a thief of time. Television is part of our culture and we all like to zone out and escape at times, but the older you become, the more you realize that one of the most valuable things in your life is time.

Once you're off that couch, probe the places you already frequent for ideas. You can volunteer through your synagogue or church or mosque. You can host a dinner party and discuss social issues. Finding your cause can be as simple as staying in your neighborhood and figuring out your neighborhood's needs. If you live near an inner city school and gardening is your passion, you can teach gardening techniques to the students to help the school become more green and beautiful instead of spending 100% of your talent and love of gardening on your own garden. If you love animals, volunteer at the local animal shelter.

No matter what, it's important to pursue new experiences. Don't use lack of money as an excuse. Seek out places you've never been to and if you have the opportunity to travel, take it. Experience different cultures and try to gain an understanding of what needs exist not only in your neighborhood, but also in the world at large. These experiences might not click with you, but they might also prove to be extremely transformative.

By the time we took our family to Africa, we'd already been involved with a number of different causes, but none of them hit all of us as personally as our exposure to the water crisis did. Our trip to Africa taught us the difference between relative poverty and absolute poverty. When our kids saw and touched life in Africa firsthand, they were better able to understand that someone in relative poverty is poor because he can't afford the latest iPhone, whereas someone in absolute poverty lives on less than a dollar a day, sleeps on hay and cow dung, and walks seven miles each day to obtain polluted water. This helps to change perspectives and when perspectives change, real change can occur.

When you seek out new experiences and walk beside the people whose problems you may want your social entrepreneurship to address, you have a better chance of finding something you can adopt as your own passion. Speak to people face-to-face and feel their cause with your own fingers. You might find the one problem that will pull at your heartstrings and your emotions. When Nina, Rachel and Bella participated in the water walk alongside the girls that were their same ages in Africa, they were hit very strongly with the realization that these girls couldn't attend school because they were fetching water while they were enjoying an education back home. This experience affected them so powerfully that they were determined to take action to help these girls.

If you're flying at forty thousand feet above the ground, you can look down on the tiny city and see the big picture, but it's difficult to identify where the specific opportunities are. In order to figure out the right problem to tackle, you have to come down to a granular or ground level. Once you reach a granular level, opportunities will start flowing toward you. If your passion is solving world hunger, then dive in and get to know the faces behind the issue. The ground level is where you'll find the first tiny niche you want to step into. It's also where you'll be better able to brainstorm social entrepreneurial ideas and be more creative. Maybe you'll come up with a type of food product that will generate a profit in the United States, and you'll be able to donate that money to an organization you've scoped out and trust. Unless you get to that granular level, you can't see the trees. All you can do is see the forest. And while the big picture is important, the big picture doesn't give you the road map that will take you to your ultimate destination.

Bead for Life is an organization that began in 2004 because three young women took a trip to Uganda. On their trip, they had a chance encounter with a Ugandan woman who rolled beads from her mud home. The three young women stopped to admire the beads, made from strips of paper, which are rolled and then protected and varnished with a shellacking to make them glossy. These beads are bright and colorful, and they can be strung together to make bracelets and necklaces. The three American women decided to buy these beads from the women in the village to sell in the United States and bring the profits back to Uganda to help these women turn their craft into a more lucrative business. So they went back home to the United States, developed a marketing strategy and then returned to Uganda to build bridges of understanding in commerce with the Ugandan women. They held classes in the village to improve the quality of the beads and inspire the women to develop more jewelry styles. The beads have sold well in the states and have turned into a successful industry for that village in Uganda. Bead for Life has now expanded by working with the shea nut industry as well. We like this story because these three women took a trip to Africa, opened up to a new experience and in doing so, discovered a life-changing passion.

You can make a list of hundreds of problems to solve. But unless you connect with it at the heart level, you won't be able to engage with the problem creatively. If you put yourself in the shoes of someone suffering because of a problem, that problem has a better chance of becoming a passion that you can open your mind to and address. It's also important that the cause you tackle is something that affects you personally because chances are that you won't be able to pursue your social entrepreneurship full time. And if you're spending your hours outside of work to invest time and energy into this endeavor, unless you wholeheartedly believe in your passion, you're at risk of burning out.

If a trip to Africa isn't feasible or isn't attractive to you, travel where you can. Instead of going to the beach during spring break, try "volunteerism" and go somewhere to volunteer for two weeks. Whatever you decide to do, get out of your comfort zone. Break your normal routine. By nature, we all fall into ruts. These ruts aren't necessarily bad, but they're stagnant and we find ourselves doing the same things over and over again. Push yourself to do something different. This is the only way we can test and explore what will make our hearts respond.

Jeff is currently at a crossroads in his work. This is a stressful time for him because there is a lot of uncertainty and lots of decisions to be made. But this is also an energizing time because there is the potential of a new idea and the potential of a new adventure at every turn. We're comfortable in this environment. We've learned to thrive in this kind of uncertainty. Many people are so uncomfortable in this environment that they do everything they can to avoid it. But the most opportunities come out of crossroads and places of decision. Jeff knows in what general direction he will take his career in two or three years. But this particular moment can veer in any one of a dozen different directions, and that's something to be excited about. Breaking up the normal routine in an established career is healthy and a great way to keep you open to new possibilities in all aspects of your life. There will definitely be some right decisions and wrong decisions, and hopefully, we'll be able to figure out how to choose the right ones. As we get older, the opportunity cost of making a wrong decision is significant, but the opportunity cost of missing the opportunity to make a decision altogether is also significant.

Making mistakes is part of the process. Fear or apprehension is also a normal reaction. But instead of fearing the consequences of a possible mistake, train yourself to be afraid of the consequences of *not* taking an opportunity. Put yourself out in the world. You don't have to know where you're going or where your experiences will take you. The problem and passion you're looking for will come to you. But you have to make the first move.

In some ways, it's easier to encourage kids to find their purpose because they're less set in their ways and more open to new experiences. Today, many parents make the mistake of pigeonholing their kids to become someone that they're inherently not. Unfortunately, many adults do this to themselves, too. It's important to begin the practice of recognizing our strengths and passions at a young age. We love the example of Craig Kielburger, who began Free the Children. His parents sat with him and his brother Marc every morning and they read the paper together. When Craig read the article about a boy his age who was murdered because he spoke out against child labor, the first sparks of Free the Children lit up inside him. Sometimes, when we find interesting news pieces on the Internet, we print them out for our kids to read. From about fifth grade onward, schools do a great job of making current events an important part of the curriculum. Only a few high schools also have a community service director who establishes a requirement of a set number of community service hours for kids before they graduate. As parents, we can teach our kids to translate these experiences into ideas for a social entrepreneurship or another kind of passion project. We've devoted a later chapter to ways to inspire your children, but for now, let's talk about practical ways to draw possible social entrepreneurial ideas from your experiences.

If you're having a hard time pinpointing your passions, take an inventory of what you do with your spare time. What you spend your spare time on may indicate where your true interests lie. Also keep a collection of your random thoughts. Write down as many thoughts as you can and then see where your mind goes and what you think regularly about. What do you like to read about? Which section of the newspaper is your favorite? What have you secretly dreamed about with regard to your work? Take copious notes about what you do and what you think about until you find a pattern that points in a specific direction.

When you're able to identify the topic that occupies your time and thoughts the most, go to the Internet and research this topic. Read as much as you can about it. Email important people who might be able to answer your questions or give you ideas. Although nine times out of ten, you won't get a response if you blindly email a high-profile person, you never know when someone will indulge you. Keep in mind Jeff's story from chapter 1 about emailing economist Jeffrey Sachs. Even if reaching out to strangers isn't your m.o., remember that leaving your comfort zone will take you far, especially in your search for your passion.

Finding your passion and then diving into it doesn't have to be an overnight endeavor. We don't advocate quitting your day job right away. Investing 100% of your time is something you can do when your idea is well under way, the logistics are in place and you feel ready. We're also not saying that you have to say no to Wall Street or to a solid paying job if you're graduating from college and you have a heart for social entrepreneurship. You can do both, and that's the beauty of the process. The idea generating process looks different for everybody. You can percolate your idea and passion for a year or for a decade or even for an entire lifetime until you've truly refined it and are ready to make a move with the project. Just because your day job isn't directly related to your passion doesn't make it wrong or irrelevant. As you use your time outside of work to develop your idea, you might even find new enthusiasm in your job because you're able to see it as a necessary means to an end instead of as the end.

Become more observant in your workplace as well. Social entrepreneurial ideas can come from the most unexpected places. TransFair USA is an organization that began in 1998 because a guy named Paul Myers worked at a regular trade agency and saw a need. He noticed an opportunity for developing countries to keep more of their income from the coffee trade in country, and recognized the difference that would make in poverty alleviation. Paul saw that when farmers don't group together to form a co-op, they end up selling their product at farm-gate pricing, which is the lowest of lows in pricing. So they make little to no profit on their goods and remain in poverty. So Paul spearheaded the fair trade movement in the coffee industry by initiating a certification program that coffee brands could subscribe to in order to ensure that more money could be retained in the communities that first produced the coffee beans. Many coffee brands have signed on to this movement because they recognize that they can differentiate themselves in the coffee market by offering a product that is socially conscious, which attracts customers. Since it first began, TransFair USA has helped more than $32 million go to farming communities that normally wouldn't have seen a cent of this money. Paul may or may not have been actively looking for a cause to attach himself to, but he kept his eyes open and paid attention well enough to find his inspiration for social entrepreneurship through his regular day job.

Probe your surroundings and the places you frequent. What needs can you identify? Can you do anything about them? Would you want to? Better World Books is a business that three friends from Notre Dame started because they wanted to sell textbooks online to make some extra cash. When they paired this business with a mission to support literacy, it exploded into a social enterprise. Since 2002, they've donated over $7.5 million dollars to funding literacy and education through the sale of used books. They also claim to have diverted more than 13,000 tons of books from landfills, which gives the organization an eco-spin and fulfills the triple bottom line that we discussed.

You can also come up with an idea by coupling something you love to do every day—such as eating meat—with a successful entrepreneurial model you admire. For example, inspired by his friend Paul Newman, Pat Boone recently launched his Pat Boone All-American Meats line of products. Pat sells high-end quality meats online and donates five percent of the revenue to different organizations that feed people at home and abroad. The focus is to help feed and sustain those in need. Through his website, you can purchase a dinner for four and you will be feeding 25 people. Pat Boone loved to eat meat, so he used his fame and his resources to address a larger social issue. Pat took Paul Newman's model and made it his own.

There are also a growing number of internet-based charity web sites where you can generate savings for your desired charity. They do this through affiliate marketing whereby, as a consumer, if you pre-sign up with the charity mall and then connect to your favorite retailer through them, your desired charity will get paid on a commission on your purchases. Good2Give is one organization that does it through the internet and Scrip is one that does it through signing up.

Stephen Covey's *7 Habits of Highly Effective People* suggests an exercise that we tried shortly after we got married. We wrote out what we wanted our future eulogy to say. This exercise forces you to think about how you want others to view your legacy once you're gone. What do you want to have accomplished by the time you leave this planet? Aside from having been a good spouse or a good parent, whose lives do you want to impact, and how? Writing your eulogy can help you determine what values and causes are important to you and what areas of interest you want to explore during your lifetime.

Begin brainstorming by allowing yourself to dream big, but also be flexible enough to adjust your dream as needed. Linda recently read a book by Rabbi Harold Kushner, who wrote *Overcoming Life's Disappointments*. We can't predict the curve balls life will throw at us, but we can prepare ourselves to be people who respond to these curve balls positively. If you've been training your entire life to be a star athlete but are injured in an accident, you can either wallow in this unfortunate incident or you can readjust your dream and become a star coach instead.

Also remember that passions and social entrepreneurships come in all shapes and sizes. You can set your eyes on solving world hunger or you can focus on feeding a small village that you have a personal connection with. Don't be overwhelmed by the number of problems there are. There will always be a cause to be addressed, and that's the beauty of this world you're diving into. Whatever you do, simply do it with your entire heart and give to your capacity.

Linda's mom raised her with the belief that you can *always* give something—whether it's your talent or your time. Every Friday, Linda's mom baked challah bread for friends and family. Everyone loved her challah bread, so during the Yom Kippur War in 1973, she and her sisters baked beautiful Jewish star challah bread to raise money for the soldiers in Israel. Somebody even purchased her bread for $5,000. Flour and water are cheap and Linda's mom loved baking. So even though their family had very little money, they thought outside of the box to find a way to give. Linda grew up putting three pennies into her small blue JNF box every day. Her mom taught her that even though she was poor, she could always spare three pennies to help someone else.

Your lack of money or even your lack of ideas should never be a roadblock that keeps you from starting a social entrepreneurship. If you don't have the capital, but you have a talent in bookkeeping, pair up with someone who has loads of capital but no desire to keep the books in a startup. There are multiple ways to get involved. Just think creatively to figure out where you can plug in your talents or your resources.

To summarize a few of the ways to find your passion we've captured them here:

- Turn misfortunes that come to you into blessings
- Put yourself out there in the world and get involved
- Trial and error—recognize that you may have to try 20 ideas to find the right one
- Volunteer
- Travel and try volunteerism
- Self-examine the things that pull at your heart
- Look at the things that you like to do with your spare time

- Read and research

- Think about needs that are unfilled in our bigger community or your local world

- Look at the values and causes that are important to you

Whether your passion is fair trade certification or literacy or water or hunger, there is a niche in the social entrepreneurial world that needs a person exactly like you. Just start small. Come down to the micro level from 40,000 feet in the sky and let your new experiences and the new people you meet trigger fresh ideas and opportunities for you. The more you seek out these experiences, the more you'll find yourself flooded with great ideas. Solving any problem begins with one step outside your comfort zone. It begins with one used book, one steak or one bottle of water. So what's your passion? What problem is calling *you*?

CHAPTER 12

The Entrepreneurial Mindset

Courage is daring to take the first step, or a different path.
It's the decision to place your dreams above your fears.
– Mark Twain –

*W*HEN YOU THINK OF entrepreneurs, which names come to mind? The word "entrepreneur" most often elicits pictures of larger-than-life, gun slinging characters such as Richard Branson or Donald Trump or Ted Turner. We imagine that social entrepreneurs are also historical giants. Mother Teresa, Muhammad Yunus and Paul Newman, for example. We tend to think that entrepreneurs are people who go from zero to hero and make a zillion dollars. Unfortunately, this means that many people also tend to believe that they could never be entrepreneurs because they think that they're nothing like those famous people, who must have that special something in their genetic makeup. But the reality is that there's an entrepreneurial mindset in *most* people. That mindset just needs to be unlocked. In this chapter, we'll talk about what that entrepreneurial mindset looks like so that you can find that entrepreneur within you.

The first step to tapping into the entrepreneurial mindset is to transform your negative "why not" thoughts into "how can I." When you have an idea, instead of listing reasons why you cannot implement that idea, practice brainstorming how you *can* do it. One of the moms from our kids' school recently started a small business on the Internet. If anyone has something to sell and wants to avoid the hassle of putting it on eBay, he or she can bring the item to this mom, who handles the entire sale, takes a commission and then sends a check. She was able to create a little business from her home because instead of remaining still and saying, "These are the reasons why I can't," she asked, "How *can* I?"

This "how can I" entrepreneurial mindset is harder to pull out from some people versus others. But once you practice entertaining your ideas and thinking of ways to execute them, you'll recognize that for every fifty ideas that you come up with, only one or two will make sense and actually be implementable. This realization will free you up to think of even more ideas, but it can also be exhausting to think of so many new ideas and start to run down each path only to find out that somebody else is already doing it or there's a fundamental flaw in the idea or it's not financially feasible. The process of idea generation and initial follow-through won't always result in the next Groupon or Facebook phenomenon, but you have to keep your creativity flowing. Keep challenging yourself to think of new ideas and always write your notes down. If you're at dinner and an idea hits you, write it on the back of a napkin. Some of the best businesses were created on the back of a napkin.

Every great entrepreneurship stems from an idea. Figure out what puts you in the frame of mind to think of ideas best. Some people are the most creative when they're out in the field of their passion. For Jeff, his ideas flow best when he goes out for a run. Some people meditate, some people read, and others get ideas in the shower. Identify the place where your mind opens up the most and keep a pad of paper near that place.

An entrepreneurial mindset is one that is creative in its idea genera-tion, but is also grounded and realistic in its plans for execution. We hear many stories about the larger-than-life exceptions—characters with lots of chutzpah who roll the dice and roll the dice again until they reach the top or hit the jackpot. These people are willing to take risks that most people can't even imagine, and because their stories are the ones that make headlines, we get a skewed idea of what it takes to be an entrepreneur. In reality, most entrepreneurs—who may not be as interesting or as colorful as the Bill

Gates and the Donald Trumps—are average people we don't read, hear, or see much about. They're normal people like you and us who come up with an idea and match it with their basic skill sets or find partners who have the skill sets they need. Then they take their shot and execute the idea. Most may not rise to the billionaire level, but they are still successful. This basic entrepreneurial mindset resides in most people. It just needs to be extracted and pulled to the surface.

Once you figure out the best way to generate your most creative ideas, you need to assess how risk-tolerant you are because the risk/reward concept plays a significant role in the entrepreneurial mindset. We all fall at different points on the continuum of risk tolerance at varying degrees of aversion to risk. Understandably, the more risk-tolerant you are, the more willing you will be to take a shot at doing something new. Younger people tend to be more risk-tolerant because people who are older often have experienced more success and therefore, they feel that they have more to lose. As we get older, we also accumulate more expenses. With kids in school and with a faster personal burn rate, older people tend to inch away from possibilities of risk.

Minimizing risk is always a smart idea, whether you're very risk-tolerant like Linda or pretty square in the middle like Jeff. We've repeated throughout the book that you don't have to quit your day job to be an entrepreneur. In fact, staying with your day job might actually inspire you to take more risks in your entrepreneurial idea because you know that you haven't cut off your main source of income.

We advocate trying lots of little experiments. For example, we talked about Bead for Life, which was started by three women who visited Uganda, became impassioned about the women they met there, and then returned home with the idea to sell the Ugandan women's beads in the United States. Their total cost of starting Bead for Life—including their initial inventory— was probably only a few thousand dollars. Without quitting their day jobs, all they had to do was carry some inventory, hold a few parties and start pitching the beads to their friends. Then as they gauged that these beads would sell, they were better able to formalize a marketing strategy, return to Uganda and create a sustainable economy through these beads.

If you know that you tend to have an aversion to risk, then you need to be wise about how to pursue your entrepreneurial ideas without increasing your burn rate. Especially in recent years, most of us are trying to tighten our belts financially, and work no longer seems to be a guarantee. So quitting a job in order to focus on an entrepreneurial project is a huge decision for the naturally risk-averse person. The first time Jeff quit a job in order to pursue an entrepreneurial idea, he made sure to save a year's worth of salary first. Then he set up his bank account so that he could send himself a pretend paycheck each month to keep himself in the mindset of an employed person who could afford the time to create and be entrepreneurial. When we don't have any money coming in and all we find ourselves doing is writing checks, our human nature tends to stifle the entrepreneurial mindset. So Jeff manipulated his aversion to risk by writing checks to himself from the money he'd saved.

No matter how risk-averse you are, it is important to keep your entrepreneurial mind running by turning your ideas into action. Whenever you have an idea, if it is feasible and you are able to think of a way to implement it, don't hesitate to act on it. Take baby steps if you have to, but make sure you're moving forward. Try one small thing at a time to turn your idea into a viable venture. Sometimes, a project like NIKA might require a large business investment. Over a three-year period, our family and the Stone family invested a significant amount of money into NIKA. But other ideas such as Bead for Life and Better World Books require far less startup costs. Ideas like these will only produce fruit if you just start doing it.

Once you take those first steps and begin to build on your entrepreneurial ideas, you'll find that you've entered the most energizing process in business. A creative spirit within you will ignite and take over when you start to take small risks and implement the ideas you have.

If you do happen to leave a job, be prepared for a bit of a culture shock. Giving up a stable job to do something entrepreneurial is like jumping off a fast-moving treadmill or train. When Jeff first left a large company to pursue his entrepreneurial endeavors, he was the president of the North and South American groups for his company. When you're the president of a group belonging to a business worth a couple hundred million dollars, suppliers, vendors, and customers alike put you on a pedestal. But the minute you remove the fancy nameplate from your office and you're on your own trying to do something, the respect you get from others is next to zero. As a budding entrepreneur, getting access to people will be very difficult in the beginning. If you've grown accustomed to working for a large company, you may sometimes feel like you're taking a step backwards.

The beginnings of the entrepreneurial process may not feel as glamorous as a position with a large company, but the entrepreneurial spirit you develop will be an asset. A generation ago, a resume gap might have looked questionable, but today, returning to a big corporate environment with a resume gap isn't a big deal. More people than ever are trying to do something entrepreneurial, and business failures aren't viewed as negatively as they have been in the past. Most of us know people who entered a dot-com business in the 90s, then became casualties when the dot-com bubble popped. One of our friends, who got caught crosswise in the dot-com crash, entered an Internet retailing business with us in 2006. This business went along swimmingly until consumer spending imploded and this business also collapsed. So although this friend has had two business failures, they've both been market timing-based failures. They could have easily been home runs that could have turned him into the next Groupon guy, but he happened to have timing work against him.

Everybody wants to invest in a winner. So if you've got a string of losers, you will have a harder time attracting capital. But if you know in your gut that your failures were timing-based, it will show in your drive and work ethic. To be honest, we would rather hire somebody who has had to make a payroll and understands what it means to have sales and supply and distribution than hire a person who has spent his or her entire career in one functional area of a well-known company. Sometimes, we even prefer that prospective employees have a number of failures under their belt because then they've had experiences that have taught them what can go wrong. These employees will know that the dew is sometimes off the roses and that the unbridled optimism of a brand new entrepreneur can run him into the ground. Working for a large company in one functional area might seem like the more attractive choice on a resume, but getting that broad experience base is important, and that experience often comes from wearing many hats in a smaller company.

People with entrepreneurial mindsets are also typically people who can look at a glass half full. They have to believe that the impossible can be possible and have faith when success or progress isn't visible. If an entrepreneur doesn't believe in her own vision, then other people will have a hard time buying into it. Pessimistic people also can't retain their entrepreneurial mindsets for very long because their negative thoughts become self-fulfilling prophecies around them and they inadvertently create their own failures.

Along these same lines, the ability to lead and inspire others is an important quality for an entrepreneur. Having some basic common sense is also important, in addition to having some specialized knowledge in the field of your pursuit. None of the qualities of an entrepreneur are qualities that you need to have exhibited in the past. They can all be acquired and practiced. But it's important to be aware of what will help you be the most productive, successful entrepreneur you can be.

One of the most essential attributes of an entrepreneurial mindset is the ability to get things done. You can have a thousand ideas, but a value for implementation needs to exist in order for any of those ideas to become a reality. Some people who are used to working for large companies often-times have great ideas, but don't know what to do with them because they've grown too comfortable having the people who work beneath them do all the dirty work. When you start your own organization, you will be the "chief," but you also have to be prepared to be an "Indian." Entrepreneurs need to be willing to roll up their sleeves to get everything and anything done. In the very beginning, you might not have the luxury of being able to pass off obnoxious and tedious tasks because you won't be able to pay somebody from the outside to come do them. We actually love this part of the entrepreneurial process. Having to do the grunt work will keep you humble and very close to and invested in the project you're developing.

Entrepreneurs must not only have the ability to get things done, but also have a knack for getting things done quickly and efficiently. We recently found out that our NIKA bottles didn't have a certification number in the state of Nevada. The certification is easy to acquire for only $83, but not having it can basically shut down our operation entirely. When Whole Foods called us because the Nevada health inspector came in and rejected our products, we had an issue at hand that needed to be dealt with as fast as possible. It would cause a huge problem for us if Whole Foods decided to pull our water bottles from its shelves. So Jeff got on the phone with the State Department of Health in Nevada and got handed off to a number of different people until he was finally able to speak to the person in charge of bottling water and come up with a solution. In certain emergency-type scenarios, outsourcing a seemingly menial task like staying on the phone with customer service may not be your best option because you might be able to accomplish something a lot quicker than a person who is newer to the game or has less at stake.

On that note, delegation is also an important art that many entrepreneurs have a hard time mastering. In certain cases, entrepreneurs need to put their team members in situations that will challenge them. This is difficult when you can't afford to fail in an entrepreneurial environment where speed, money and time are crucial. It will be difficult for you to delegate tasks to others because there is always the question of whether those other people on your team are as invested as you are in your idea. A difference in work ethic will also be hard to navigate as you practice delegating responsibilities. When we were younger, Saturdays were a given workday for most offices and businesses. Our generation believes that the secret to a successful entrepreneurial 40-hour workweek is to work seventy hours. Young people seem to have a harder time grasping this concept, which makes it difficult to assess what tasks you can delegate to them and ensure that they get done.

In order to delegate well, entrepreneurs have to be an accurate judge of character. Assess the capacities and skills of your team members. If a younger person can accomplish something faster on a computer, it's better to delegate that task. And if you're worried about the final result, you can always monitor the work and tweak it if you have to. To be an efficient entrepreneur, figure out what truly needs your personal touch. You don't need to deal with every client or customer, but there might be a few key individuals whom you'll want to interact with personally. On the same token, you don't need to micromanage every detail. The entrepreneurial mindset must be able to discern when it is more efficient for someone else to handle a task.

We recently had a glitch with our Internet ordering system, which wasn't effectively charging people's credit cards. We delegated the problem to one of our team members who has been working with the marketing firm and understands the technology. But he didn't understand the urgency of the situation, so when the marketing end said, "We're working on it," he took it on faith, told us, "They're working on it," and let a few days slip by. A few days turned into a few more days, which turned into a week of missing Internet orders during the holiday season. This was a situation that we could have kept a better eye on while delegating or could have done a better job on ourselves. A week was much too long to let this problem go unfixed. Entrepreneurs must have a bias for action, and we have to know when our team members will step up to their delegated task with that same bias for action, and also be able to determine when they might not.

Self-confidence is another important characteristic of the entrepreneurial mindset. Self-confidence goes hand-in-hand with perseverance. We all have our insecurities, and nobody expects you to be a 10 out of 10 on the self-confidence continuum. But you should at least be right of center so that you don't back down at the smallest sign of trouble. When you embark on an entrepreneurship, new information will come at you daily to test whether your project is headed in the right direction. In the bottled water market, we might discover that there is another socially conscious bottled water company out there and we'll have to ask ourselves whether we want to be just another face in a crowd of these bottled water companies. Or we might hear that Coca-Cola has just developed a plant-based bottle that some say will take over the market from an environmental standpoint. Any piece of information like that can shake your foundation. And in order to remain in the game and not falter at the first sign of direct competition, you have to have confidence. Your confidence is what will be the lighthouse or the beacon on the hill that will guide you even if you get hit off course.

Insecure people or people with low confidence will always find reasons to quit. Sometimes, there is a time when the wise choice *is* to quit, but the entrepreneurial mind doesn't quit easily. In the beginning of any entrepreneurial process, you will have recurring thoughts such as, "Oh no, somebody else is doing the same thing," or "Somebody is doing this cheaper," or "Somebody is doing this better." We were recently talking with a young woman and co-founder of sOccket, the soccer ball that can be used to generate electrical power. She was struggling a bit because their soccer ball weighs 22 ounces and a normal soccer ball weighs 15 ounces. Their soccer ball also costs four times the price of a normal soccer ball, and isn't quite as durable. They have the choice to brainstorm how to move forward or to quit. It's a great product and our advice was for them to persevere, keep the faith and continue putting one foot in front of the other. The difference between winning and losing is sometimes so razor thin.

If an entrepreneur is self-confident, he can instill that confidence in his team and inspire everyone else to follow through and tackle difficult circumstances head-on. This is important because the last thing you want to do after spending so much of your time and probably some of your limited capital resources is quit and then look back five years later and say, "I wish I would have kept going a little longer." Your self-confidence will give you the perseverance you need to fight the good fight and give it your all.

If you're going to leave the battlefield, you must be able to look at yourself in the mirror and say, "I know I tried to make this thing work as best as I could, but I gave it my all and it's not meant to be." Too many entrepreneurs make the mistake of throwing in the towel way too early.

When you face the temptation to give up, consider this quote: "He failed in business in '31. He was defeated for state legislature in '32. He tried another business in '33. It failed. His fiancée died in '35. He had a nervous breakdown in '36. In '43, he ran for Congress and was defeated. He tried again in '48, and was defeated again. He tried running for the Senate in '55. He lost. The next year he ran for Vice President and lost. In '59 he ran for the Senate again and was defeated. In 1860, the man who signed his name A. Lincoln was elected the 16th President of the United States. The difference between history's boldest accomplishments and its most staggering failures is often, simply, the diligent will to persevere."

That "diligent will to persevere" is certainly an integral part of the entrepreneurial mindset. That indomitable will can be shaped if you possess some of the other foundations of an entrepreneurial mindset—a positive outlook and an unshakable confidence. Remember that almost anybody can be an entrepreneur. You just have to be willing to stand up against your negative thoughts.

The entrepreneurial mindset is one that understands that failure is okay. In fact, failure is a good and necessary part of this adventure. Like we've said before, the businesses that have failed are the ones that have taught us the most. As long as you have a teachable spirit and you learn from each of your mistakes, your failures can be refurbished to become your greatest assets. The entrepreneurial mindset is one that is creative enough and confident enough to turn almost every negative situation or thought into a blessing in disguise. It possesses the perseverance of Abraham Lincoln and dares to expect success even when all the signs point in the opposite direction.

The Entrepreneurial mindset can be summarized with the following principles:

- Recognize that the basic entrepreneurial mindset exists in most of us

- Think "how can I" versus "why I can't"

- Figure out what type of activity puts you in the best frame of mind to be creative

- Understand your personal risk tolerance perspective

- Try lots of tiny little experiences to better understand your mindset

- Act on your ideas, even if it is with baby steps

- A mindset that is all about the ability to get things done

- Self-confidence, at least a decent knowledge

- The diligent will to persevere

CHAPTER 13

Teaching Your Children to Give Back

Give a man a fish, feed him for a day,
teach him how to fish, feed him for a lifetime.
– Lao Tzu –

*T*HE SKILL SETS AND traits that we explored in the earlier chapters on leadership and entrepreneurship are also important in the family setting. We've always tried to build a good foundation in our children through education, just as Linda's mother did by teaching her to put three pennies into her charity box every day. Since our children were little, we always talked about doing good deeds whenever we had our children's attention. We would use car rides as sermon time to talk to them about giving back to whatever capacity that they could understand, whether it is sitting with somebody that's new and doesn't know anybody or simply looking for somebody to help. We stressed the obligation of giving back and the power of giving to somebody's capacity, whether it is your money, your talent, or your time. It was critical to build this foundation early to awaken the sense of compassion that would stay with them for the rest of their lives.

As parents, it was our responsibility to lead by example. Children, especially at a young age, always watch what you do as a parent. How you treat the homeless person on the street. How you treat the Salvation Army lady as you're walking out of the store. How you treat people will ultimately shape how your kids treat those people. We all have negative biases that we pick up over the course of our lives. We'll say to ourselves, "Oh, don't give money to that homeless guy because he'll just go buy alcohol." Or, "Don't stop and talk to that person because she'll just try to sell you something." We recognized this and actively tried to lay down our built-in negative biases. It's important to shift our paradigms as adults because then our children will see this and respond to it. If we do nothing and hold on to the negative biases we accumulate over our lifetimes, the odds are that our kids will adopt the same mindset. So we've made an effort to expose our kids to more positive ways of thinking from an early age.

It's important to cultivate the behavior of wanting to give and create a culture of giving in the family. Rather than simply talking to them, we tried to engage our children and get them involved early in the process instead of just telling them what to do. One way we accomplished this was through family and individual mission statements. Every year between Rosh Hashanah and Yom Kippur, we would take time to write our mission statements. We would set aside time as a family to reflect on what we felt we did well this year and what we each needed to work on. This time was great because it afforded us an opportunity to write down and reflect, begin a clean slate, and work on our goals during the New Year. This not only helped focus our attention to becoming better people, but also really brought us closer as a family. We made sure that our children came to the table with different ideas and we found that the holidays became opportunities for teachable moments with our children.

We made sure that each mission statement we wrote always included some kind of charitable focus. It could be something really small or something bigger and more ambitious. Each year, the children would put down their suggestions and we, as a family, would incorporate them into our mission statements. This way, our approach wasn't simply top-down, but also very much bottom-up with their involvement in it. It allowed them to be much more engaged and hands on with their ideas.

This is also a strategy that our community service program leader, Susie Nordenger, employs frequently to engage the children. We mentioned her earlier in the book and what she does with children is really amazing. She lets the kids take the lead in community service by allowing them to pick the project, figure out how to raise the funds for it, and then execute the plan. The children are engaged in driving the project from start to finish. Then, at the end of each year, the kids reflect on what worked, what didn't, what they could have done better, and leave notes for the community service people next year.

We can't stress enough how important it is to involve children in the entrepreneurial process. When kids are passionate, their passion spreads to other kids, to their parents, and the entire endeavor just grows and grows exponentially. When the kids talk passionately about the cause, they speak from the heart, and they get everybody around them inspired and motivated to want to go out and help.

As parents, we all have a vision of what we want our kids to be doing, but in reality, our kids are only going to gravitate to what they want to do. It's natural instinct as parents to want the very best for our children. Parents tend to want their kids to be the next Michael Jordan or the next Bill Gates. And sometimes, we tend to push, push, and push in those directions. Our son, Joshua, is exceptional in terms of capabilities and talent. But he will occasionally come home with an oddball thought on what he wants to do, and sometimes, we think that he might be underselling himself in some particular areas. But you've got to let your kids explore different ideas because in reality, they may not be the next Bill Gates. They may not be the next Michael Jordan. Instead, you should want them to be good human beings who give back. Let them explore to find their passions because you never know what it's going to be. Children may do what we tell them to do for a little bit, but that won't be sustainable if it doesn't come from the kids. But if they can match their passions with their vocation, they'll be successful in life.

We've tried to expose our children to different experiences in order to see what they gravitate toward. When our children were young, we tried to donate or volunteer our family's time at various events. We took them to events where they could experience the act of giving—whether it was rummaging through closets to gather old clothes to donate or doing the canned food drive during Thanksgiving. Every Thanksgiving, our schools run a canned food drive for those less fortunate, and our kids have always been very active in supporting this cause. The Wednesday morning before Thanksgiving, television crews come in and the kids get to see on television the reward and the impact of an activity where they've invested their time.

We've also tried to develop a philanthropic commitment through experiences. We took our kids to Ethiopia and Kenya and saw firsthand the level of poverty that exists in the world. Our kids saw other kids walking seven miles to get polluted water, missing the opportunity to go to school and marrying at twelve, thirteen, or fourteen years old. Most kids learn better experientially than they do from just reading a book. The Africa trip provided our kids with such a tangible experience that when they got back home, they had a whole different perspective on what to do with an empty bottle of water. Our kids didn't want to throw it out into recycling. Instead, they wanted to save it because they saw the kids in Africa use a plastic water bottle as a soccer ball. Obviously not everybody can take their kids to Africa. But anybody can go down to a homeless shelter and nudge their kids out of their comfort zones. Interacting with people who don't look healthy or who might smell can have a large impact in the children's lives.

Expose your children to a wide variety of experiences. It doesn't necessarily have to be service or charity oriented, but when you find something that your kid is interested in, spark or ignite that passion. Children will not become charitably oriented toward a cause that they don't really care about. A passion may be horses for our daughter or basketball for our son. When you find that passion, spur it on and explain to your kids that they can use this also to do something pretty cool for others. Tie together their interests with the concepts of giving back.

Even if you're not that involved with charities or service work, you can expose your kids to new experiences through your church or synagogue or another community service organization with a strong giving component. Engage your children in a community service function at the school they attend. Have the community service director of the school become familiar with your child so that he or she can match service opportunities with your child's interests. Starting early allows your kids to build a growing relationship with community service and also helps them find their true passions, which is what's really important. The key is to start early, get them involved and see what sticks.

Even if kids don't have exposure to giving at a young age, it only takes one person to ignite that spirit of compassion inside them. There's a great film called, *Homeless to Harvard: The Liz Murray Story*, which profiles a young woman whose parents were drug addicts in New York and the system allowed them to continue to be on welfare. Her mom ended up dying of AIDS in the hospital and even though she and her sister became homeless, they survived. Liz was on the street for two years, literally lived on the subway, yet still did really well in high school. One of her teachers saw how brilliant she was and encouraged her to keep going. Liz eventually applied to Harvard and she got in. We heard her tell her story firsthand at a leadership summit and it was truly inspiring. It took only one person in her life to help her get through her circumstance. And now Liz Murray really gives back. She goes around the country sharing her story and does incredible charity work. She had no guidance on giving back, but learned because someone gave to her. She realized the importance of giving and has dedicated her life to helping communities. We need to continually tell our children about stories like these to inspire them.

When your children gravitate toward something, work with them to go a little deeper with that particular thing. Involve them with organizations related to their interests. Then your children can develop relationships within these organizations so that their involvement sticks with them. When your children don't end up on the periphery of the organizations, the charity or cause becomes something far more intimate and personal. If they start young and get involved as a hobby at first, they can work their way up over the years and by the time they're in high school, they can play a significant role in that organization or cause. Have your kids intern in more specific areas of interest as they get older. If they're interested in poverty alleviation, for example, network through a non-governmental organization and help them get a job or internship for a summer to see if that passion really resonates with them. This not only can help them hone in on their cause, but can also be a great supplement for college applications and for their future.

As children get older, teaching them about entrepreneurship is also really important. Our daughter, Nina, said that not one of her 120 classmates wants to go into business after high school. This lack of interest in business may be partly due to the fact that they go to a fairly liberal prep school where kids tend to go into advanced education and liberal colleges. But what is interesting is that Nina said two freshmen who recently visited from college—one, a pre-med student and the other, pre-law—are now interested in starting businesses and potentially switching careers from medicine and law to business.

The Facebook phenomenon and *The Social Network* movie have certainly motivated a lot of young people to think that they can also create a lot of value. Now Mark Zuckerberg is talking about giving back half of his net worth over the remainder of his life. Kids are now starting to be attracted to becoming socially conscious while also being entrepreneurial. It's a shame that our school systems aren't teaching kids more about business. There are talented kids in middle and high schools who have never considered business. So as parents, we've got to educate our kids on the positive aspects of business and entrepreneurship.

A critical part of the foundation that you also want to lay early in your child's life is the value of money. A friend of ours started a website called Three Jars, which teaches younger kids about allowances. The basic concept is the idea of having three jars: save, spend, and share. Parents set an amount for allowance each week. Kids then get IOUs from parents to spend in each jar. For example, parents can say they want to give $10 a week to their kids. The parents and the kids can then allocate a percentage basis between save, spend, and share.

Parents can also set an interest rate for the save jar. The jars teach children not only the concept of saving, but also the importance of budgeting money and the importance of donating. Kids can allocate the funds from the share jar to whatever charities they desire. They can watch their money grow in the save jar. And they can make withdrawals from the spend jar by making requests for cash from their parents. This concept helps parents discuss money management with kids at an early age. Oftentimes, business and money are perceived negatively, but it's really important to teach our children the concepts of saving and sharing. They manage to figure out the spending part pretty well on their own.

Another great website and organization that teaches kids about the power and value of money is Kiva. It's basically a microfinance website that has hundreds of different causes, charities, and small time entrepreneurs from all over the world, primarily the developing world. On that site, you make small loans of nominal amounts of money, anywhere from a few bucks to a couple hundred dollars. The loan then has a payback methodology. You may loan $200 to somebody to buy a goat. Then when that person pays back the loan, you're able to use more money to invest in other projects, which you can see through graphics and charts. The payback ratios on the site are very, very high. This site is great for kids who don't have a lot of money because if you only have $10 but you team up with four people who each also have $10, you can lend $50 to a woman to buy knitting material to knit hats and scarves. Kids can directly feel the benefits of giving through this website because they get to see the project, see the progress on the work, and touch and feel what nominal amounts of money can do.

It's important to teach our kids to take ownership of their giving. Our society always stresses that we have certain rights to things, but there are also obligations that come with those rights and privileges. We have an obligation to other people. We always tried to make sure our kids understood how our democratic capitalist society is built compared to a traditional socialist society. In a traditional socialist society, the government provides the care and charity work while the taxpayers fund the government at high tax rates.

A capitalist society government also does some of that, but most of the giving comes from private individuals since we are taxed at much lower rates. American capitalism is great because we can be in charge of allocating our donation capital instead of having the government take more taxes out of our wallet and then dole it out. We made sure our children understood that because our economy and our society are not built on relying solely on the government, each one of us has an obligation to give back. It's important to realize that we pay lower taxes compared to the rest of the world, which comes with an obligation to give back in whatever capacity we can.

Gandhi says, "Whatever you do will be insignificant, but it is very important that you do it." We've shared the story of Linda's mother, who had no money when the Yom Kippur War broke out in 1973, but baked challah bread to sell for donations to the war. It's important to stress to our kids that it's not about how much you give, but about realizing that every effort makes an impact.

Another great example of giving to your capacity is a mother at our school who really wanted to do the Africa trip with NIKA. She has three kids and she told us that her family wanted to join the Africa trip, but they were struggling because her husband had just lost his job. They even had to pull two of their kids out of our school. So we told her, "Your kids are still a little too young for that trip, and they really will not get as much out of it as you would like. But if you wait two more years, then they'll be the perfect age. So why don't you get a big jar, and every time your family has extra change, put that change in the jar. We promise you'll be surprised that by the time they're old enough, you'll have the trip paid for." She loved the idea. We often don't realize what we take for granted or what we discard in our society, because we are, thankfully, a society of wealth. But saving those pennies in jars can make a huge difference. Over the course of years, they can turn into thousands of dollars and have a really meaningful impact.

These examples also help kids overcome discouragement and the feeling that they can't make a meaningful difference in the world. Abraham

Joshua Heschel said, "I may not be able to change the world, but I'm not going to let the world change me." Reinforce in your children the idea of giving to one's capacity no matter what goes on in the larger world. Remind them that ordinary people do extraordinary things. We have to teach our kids that they don't have to end world hunger. They don't have to end war. They don't have to end animal cruelty. But if they simply act within their capacity and help save one dog or if they donate $20 to bring clean water to one person for a lifetime, that's making a difference. As parents, teachers and professionals, we have to keep kids committed to the idea that they don't have to change the world. All they have to do is change one life. Then if they change one life, they can change a second life, then a third life. Pretty soon, you're changing a sea of lives.

With the Internet today, paradigms are not only shifting, they're also being shattered. Our kids are being raised in an environment where there aren't any limitations. Just on Facebook alone, there are over 25,000 different causes that you can like or dislike simply by clicking a thumbs up or a thumbs down. There's a whole social media movement that allows kids to see causes all the time. While most aren't going to resonate, there will be some that get their hearts going, and those are the ones we need to nurture and flourish.

When we give, we almost always gain more than we give. So once they understand that positive feeling one time, they tend to want to do it again and again because giving makes them feel so good. Then it just becomes a matter of looking for opportunities to do good deeds. And once you begin looking, you suddenly find them everywhere.

Parents have to maintain realistic expectations. Kids might have great ideas of grandeur that they forget about. Don't let them or yourself feel like that's a failure. When our children are young, they're not going to be committed to everything. They just don't have the attention span to follow through. And attention is not something you can force. Our responsibilities and expectations should only be to instill the idea of giving back, and stir the entrepreneurial thought processes in our children. Once you stir that, they will continue to think of ideas. We tell our kids every day to think outside the box as they do everyday tasks. We ask, "What would make your life easier?" and push them to think of one creative idea.

Give your children the chance to explore their entrepreneurial sides on their own, and you might be surprised by their ideas. One night, we were eating tacos at dinner and our son Jacob came up with one of the funnier, more interesting ideas. He said, "I want to invent Taco Tape."

We asked, "What's that?"

And Jacob said, "My tacos always fall apart! I want to invent a tape that you can use to wrap your tacos and eat, but doesn't taste like anything." We encouraged the idea, so now Jacob thinks about new applications for his taco tape every time we eat a messy food. We are trying to help him develop this into a viable product. However, even more important is the concept that Jacob is wired to think of creative ideas and hopefully one day, one of those ideas can turn into something significant. Parenting with social entrepreneurship in mind is really about inspiring kids to want to think in new ways and nurturing them to be intellectually curious.

Just talk to your kids. Ask them what bothers them in the world. Then really listen and find some basic websites or books for them to look at to learn more about the issue they discussed. But you also don't want to give your children too much to do or you'll overwhelm them. Even to this day, our children come up with great ideas and we're always supportive about getting behind their ideas, but their appetite is always bigger than their stomach. They tend to want to bite off more than they can chew. At the end of the day, they've also got school commitments so we're careful not to over-commit them to too many things. You have to constantly walk them through, help them focus their talents, and allow their passions to lead their lives.

Give your kids the room to run with their passions. This will make them feel empowered as they have full ownership of their endeavors. They won't think it's mom's or dad's idea being pushed on them. They're going to think it's their idea. And remember to give them room to fail. Even if their website or product launch goes nowhere, you'll be able to talk about that as a teaching point for years to come. The most important thing is to stir something in the recesses of their minds so they'll want to continue both the charity side of things and the entrepreneurial side.

Plant the seeds that will grow into a deep desire for social entrepreneurship one day. Encourage your children to look at the world in a different light. Create the bug that will make them want to be entrepreneurs. Instill the bug that will make them want to give back. But understand that these things won't happen overnight. Plant these seeds early on so they can be harvested and shift their paradigms later in life. Maybe at 20 years old, they'll suddenly want to take a trip to experience something more.

There's really no way to fail as a parent if you do these things because at a minimum, your children will help people, and at a maximum, they'll get something great off the ground. Changing the way your children look at the world will change the way you do, too. It will change the way you look at your role as both a parent and a contributor to society. There's really no downside. So create a culture of giving. Set the stage for your children's futures in a powerful way.

Keys ways to teach your kids to give back:

- Cultivate the culture of giving within your family
- Engage your children early in the process
- Together with your family, write your family mission each year
- Involve your children in the entrepreneurial process
- Help match your child's passion with their vocation
- Expose your kids to as many new experiences as possible
- Empower them to make their own decisions, even if it may lead to a setback
- Internalize the obligation to give to one's capacity and to give back
- Ask your kids what really bothers them in the world

CHAPTER 14

Be the Change!

If not now, when? If not you, who?
– Rabbi Hillel –

*M*AHATMA GANDHI SAID, "Be the change you wish to see in the world," Imagine the possibilities if everybody lived by both of Gandhi's and Hillel's quotations!

One of Linda's favorite Jewish prayers is the *Shehecheyanu*, which is a blessing that celebrates the significance of the present moment. We believe in taking full advantage of every moment because there is no way to predict what tomorrow will bring. It's possible to become overwhelmed as you imagine the changes that you wish to see in the world or list the global issues that you wish to see solved. But don't resign yourself to saying, "I can't fix it." The size of a problem or the apparent impossibility of a situation doesn't absolve you from doing your part to become engaged and do something to implement what small changes you *can* make. Every great idea begins with one person. If not you, who? If not now, when?

Our hope for this book is not only to share the NIKA story, but also to inspire you to start running with your own social entrepreneurial ideas. We want to create a space for people like you who are—or will be—creating similar socially-motivated business ventures. We recently received an email from a budding social entrepreneur who was referred to us by a Michigan State University student who told him about NIKA and said that we would be great resources for his questions. He wrote us the following:

"Mr. Church, let me start by saying I'm a big fan of NIKA and your efforts as a social entrepreneur. I'm writing you today to tell you about a socially responsible company that I am currently starting. I'm starting a knit hat brand that donates a percentage of revenue from each sale of hats to manufacturing the distribution of protein supplements to developing nations. Protein deficiency is one of the world's largest problems and nobody knows about it. Our goal is to market high quality, stylish hats to Americans in order to raise awareness of this problem and fund the eradication of this deficiency through mass supplementation."

He goes on to say, "I was wondering if you could give me advice on raising capital for my company. I'm just finishing a business plan, and will be approaching investors in January. I've attached the executive summary of my business plan, which includes more information on our cause as well as our operations. Thank you very much for your time and consideration."

In our eyes, if the NIKA story is spreading to entrepreneurs like this young man, then we've reached one of our most important goals, which is to create grounds for other likeminded people who want to be world changers. We want to leverage ourselves in a broader arena than just over our company, and reach as many people as possible. We love emails like this one because it reinforces exactly what we aim to do.

The NIKA story can be your story. Are you somebody who wants to give back to the world? Are you also somebody who wants to make a buck? You can do both. And you can do it *now*.

We've said this before, and it's worth repeating: you can continue on your current path—whether you're in business school or at a job you've had for fifteen years—while you simultaneously percolate your social entrepreneurial idea. You don't have to put your life passion on hold. And you don't have to give up your stable income. Instead of playing an extra round of golf a week, allocate that time to working with troubled youth. Or take a trip. Volunteer. Start a website. Start a blog about the cause you're interested in. Then when you've picked up some business lessons and you have the financial wherewithal to launch your social entrepreneurship, you will have momentum as you go forth.

The danger of putting your passion on hold for too long is that the more established you are in your life, the farther you will have to fall if your entrepreneurial idea doesn't go as planned. So if you truly have a desire to start something, do it sooner than later. When you get used to making more money and catering to a higher cost of living with a family to take care of, these blessings become an encumbrance. A set of golden handcuffs. Taking risks only gets harder as you age. We have several massively successful friends, many of which have hated their career choices since day one. They are not living out their passions, and the challenge for them is to figure out how to jump into a passion knowing that there is a possibility that they might fail and have a long way to fall. Don't quit your day job, but don't hesitate too long to start.

As you start your social entrepreneurship, remember to stay grounded and remain focused on why you've adopted your cause. Beware of the ego. Many entrepreneurs let their egos get in the way of their progress. Instead of trying to provide a service and address a problem in the world, a person with an inflated ego can turn his or her social entrepreneurship into a self-focused, unproductive project. Remember that the success of any social entrepreneurship depends on a multitude of factors. Your idea may be great and you may bring a number of talents and gifts to the table, but timing also plays an important role. Success has a lot to do with being at the right place at the right time. It's important to remember this when your business does well so that you don't develop an ego that could become your blind side. This will keep you in check if you happen to embark on a second or third entrepreneurial project. We've come to realize that we were no different in our four business wins than we were in our two business losses. If we are honest with ourselves, we can say that timing, opportunity and luck had a hand in whether any of our businesses succeeded or failed.

If you are grounded in your vision and you keep your ego in check, then others—potential investors or potential clients—will feel more comfortable signing on to your social entrepreneurship. An enthusiastic entrepreneurial spirit is great because it will inspire people to believe in you, but it's also important to have reasonable business projections. Try to present your social entrepreneurship in the way that you would want someone to present it to you. Then you will be able to predict their reactions and questions and address the fundamental issues that might be their hot buttons in that initial presentation. Some businesses get lucky and swing from zero dollars to $100 million in revenue in the first three years. But it's important to be realistic. Remember The Rule of Two and expect startups to take double the time and double the cost. A growth of 10 to 20% per year is something to be appreciated.

Several years ago, we heard Dennis Prager's father, Max Prager, being interviewed on the radio. Dennis said to his father, "Dad, you've always been a happy guy. You've always done well. What's your secret?"

Max Prager replied, "I live by three words: Attitude, attitude and gratitude."

We love this idea, and we've tried to internalize it in our children because it's simple, easy to memorize and makes a huge difference on your quality of life. Your attitude and your outlook on life will affect the way you choose to address problems and difficult situations when they arise. Everything is about perspective. When we read newspaper headlines, we can choose to become bitter or choose to become inspired to act. People who practice gratitude also tend to keep their egos in check and tend to be happier. And happy people are less likely to be overly self-focused and more likely to become engaged with the world and move in a forward direction.

Our son recently underwent knee surgery. During one of the physical therapy sessions, the doctor drained the fluids from our son's knee, which put him in a lot of pain. It happened to be an awful, rainy day and he was growing increasingly frustrated as he tried to get in the car without adding to his pain. But before we could say anything to him, he turned to us and said, "I know, I know. 'Attitude, attitude and gratitude.'"

Our son was going through a lot of pain, but he told us that he'd been thinking about his friend Thomas, who has been battling cancer for the past year. Thomas has had his hips removed and the doctors have excised several tumors from his body. And our son said, "I really have no room to complain compared to what Thomas has been through." This is exactly the mindset that we want our kids to have. Life hands lemons to a lot of people. Everyone can sit around and feel sorry for whatever situation he or she is in, but there is always somebody in worse shape. Instead of wallowing in our misfortunes, we need to practice finding things in our lives that we can be grateful for.

If you practice this "attitude, attitude, gratitude" mindset in your everyday life, it will be second nature to employ that same positive mindset when you embark upon a social entrepreneurial activity. Remember that you're not immune to failure, but the same is true for everybody else so don't let the possibility of failure affect your attitude. An uncurbed ego can be detrimental, but being overly insecure or feeling inferior is also a problem. It's important to have a can-do attitude from the beginning and believe that you *can* win so that you're not defeated from the get-go.

When you do something entrepreneurial, you'll find a reason to quit at every turn. The young entrepreneur who emailed us about his hat company wants to raise $100,000. He could have a really difficult time raising this money and that will test his drive and his passion. When his company and his idea are tested, will he pack it in, put the company on hold for the rest of his life and return to what he did before? Or will he decide that even if he doesn't get the money, he will continue with his idea and pare it down to comply with a much smaller budget? If he doesn't raise his capital, but is serious about this passion, he could purchase a few hats, set them up on a website and start selling them one at a time that way. Every project can always be scaled back rather than abandoned. The success of your entrepreneurship will depend on how well you handle adversity. Most entrepreneurs have a willingness to persevere because they believe in their cause or in their business and are determined to make it happen one way or another. When you get cold water thrown on your idea, will you make ice cubes with it or will you pitch the tent and go home?

We understand that it's not easy to make significant changes in your life. A little anxiety is to be expected as you venture out of your comfort zone. Most people who are about to begin an entrepreneurship are terrified of altering their regular life course even though they appear to be wearing their game faces. It's the norm—not the exception—to feel nervous. You will experience a powerful energy when you embrace that feeling and push yourself to continue in spite of it.

Ordinary people can do extraordinary things. You can, too. Just get up off your couch and take your first step. That first step will be your hardest step, but in some ways, also the most important. Think back to the group of interviewed senior citizens who said that they wished they had taken more risks in their professional careers. Learn from these people who have been there so that you don't look back and have regrets. Hold on to the notion that in a hundred years, your bank account, the car you drove and the kind of house you had won't matter, but what will matter is whether you made a difference in the life of someone.

The Talmud says that if you save one life, then you save the world. You *can* make a difference, but you don't have to eat the whole elephant at once. Take one bite at a time. Nobody expects you to solve the world's issues so don't put that pressure on yourself. Realistically, you're not going to solve world hunger. You're not going to end the water crisis or stop animal cruelty, and that's okay. If you try to jump from A to Z, you'll throw your arms up in the air and decide that the task is too daunting. You have to work through the alphabet, one step at a time. But note the sense of urgency. Acting out of the box will only get harder, so if you have an entrepreneurial idea, implement it now. You might even find that it energizes and motivates you enough to steer your life on a whole different path.

Creating your own mission will also be easier if you have a good handle on your beliefs and principles. Know and be able to articulate your life philosophy. Know what kind of person you want to become. Then act as though you were already that person that you aspire to be and you'll find yourself becoming that person. When you know what you believe in and who you want to be, you'll rely less on other people to produce change and instead, take the reigns yourself.

Some families at our school compare themselves to the more afflu-ent, well-known families and say, "Well, we can't give to charities like they do. And if they give, then there's no need for us to give." That mentality is also what tempts the people who say that they don't have to worry about social issues because the government will solve our problems for us. That's the absolute wrong attitude. We all have an obligation to give according to our capacity. The bottom line is that we are our brothers' keepers. We have a social obligation to take care of each other in whatever way we can. Whether your capacity is starting a social entrepreneurship or being avail-able to one friend in need, the important thing is that you don't remain passive, but go forth and do something.

The government is available to handle certain issues, but everyone has to play a part in taking care of his or her community. The trend these days is to label capitalists as corrupt, greedy, evil people. But the truth is that all humans and human-run organizations have the potential to be corrupt, greedy and evil. Governments included. So sticking negative labels on such a broad group of people will only limit your ability to see how they can be used to benefit society. It makes more sense to trust individuals to have the compassion to take care of their neighbors and to trust entrepreneurs to solve problems because that's what they're good at. So instead of jumping on a political bandwagon and writing off capitalism as an evil entity, chal-lenge yourself to extract its positive attributes and use them to your benefit.

Too many well-intentioned young people grab on to trendy non-profit philosophies and shy away from business because they've been taught that greed is evil and that wanting more is bad. Many kids take these anti-capitalistic ideas for the gospel because some college professors and even movies such as *Wall Street* reinforce these ideas. Sure, wanting material things just for the sake of wanting material things might be unhealthy if you're not a grounded person, but too much of any good thing can't be bad. The fact is that wanting more is not only good, but also necessary. The people who want more are the ones who find cures for diseases. They're the ones who invent the conveniences we can no longer live without. Wanting more is the essence of the entrepreneurial drive to innovate. We urge you now to marry that drive with a passion for social issues so that we can rev up our economy again while making a difference in the world.

If you buy into the idea that capitalism equals greed, then you cheat yourself out of the opportunity to have a great social entrepreneurial experience. You're also cheating a lot of people in developing nations out of the help you could provide for them, and also out of the opportunity to become entrepreneurs themselves. If you can define your principles and your passions for social well-being and entrepreneurship, and then draw on those principles as you make life decisions, you will be more balanced and focused as you try to make a difference in the world. Douglas MacArthur once said, "A true leader has the competence to stand alone, the courage to make tough decisions, and the compassion to listen to the needs of others. He does not set out to be a leader, but becomes one by the equality of his actions and the integrity of his intent. In the end, leaders are much like eagles. They don't flock. You find them one at a time." Being aware of the needs around you and maintaining your integrity will automatically make you a leader and entrepreneur.

As you start implementing your social entrepreneurial idea, write a few notes to yourself about who you are and who you want to be. Define your personal mission and then act accordingly. Even the smallest action can make a huge difference. So start small and do something—even if that's the only action you take.

Social entrepreneurship and charitable giving have become micro trends in the United States. Our goal is to use the NIKA story and this book to usher those trends into a macro wave. The more people talk about social entrepreneurships and the more they entertain the possibilities, the closer we will be to changing the world.

Americans are raised with an appreciation for capitalism and innovative thinking. Americans are also encouraged to give back to their communities. Social entrepreneurship has entered the conversation to bring good news to Americans who have a passion for both; making money and giving money away are not mutually exclusive. The for-profit and non-profit worlds are thinking outside of the box to merge together and create more sustainable ways of addressing the world's problems. Your part can be as big or as small as you feel comfortable.

The ways we can give back to our communities are endless. Simply look around you for inspiration. Help a neighbor. Get involved with a shelter or religious organization. If you're inspired and you do your small act with a lot of passion, then that small act will evolve into more small acts and you will find yourself becoming that change you want to see.

Do you want to leave a legacy? Do you want to make a difference in the lives of others? If you do, then embrace the exciting changes that lie ahead for you. Understand your risks, find your passions, then take the lessons you've gathered from this book, hold on to a few of your favorite inspirational stories and run ahead at full force! No matter how far along you are in the social entrepreneurial process, make a move. And enjoy every move that follows. Laugh a little. Or laugh a lot! You don't have to know exactly where this journey will take you. Learn to love that mystery.

So will you join this wave of social entrepreneurships? As you sit on your surfboard and you see the wave approach, you have two choices. You can either have the wave roll right by you or you can paddle out, get up on your board and ride the wave.

We began this book by asking, "Can a bottle of water save the world?" If a bottle of water can save one person, then it has already begun to save the world. If your social entrepreneurial idea changes you, then you've already begun to change the world. So what are you waiting for? Dream big. And start small. But start.

Appendix

Entrepreneur Self Exam

$\mathcal{B}$EING AN ENTREPRENEUR IS an incredible adventure. While it's risky it can be an amazing life journey. This tool is meant to be "a self examination into what areas you may want to focus on strengthening prior to embarking on your adventure."

There are no right or wrong answers, however if you see sections or areas where you are low relative to others, you may want to spend time shoring up the lower areas.

We have found that the areas of 1) Personal Experience; 2) Ideas; 3) Finances and 4) Outside Support seem to encompass the main areas that are important to being an entrepreneur.

At our workshop at the conference we will talk through this and walk through a live example of a volunteer.

As an example, we've completed one section as if an aspiring entreprenuer had in fact done a venture on their own before. However, they have never worked in the area that they are specifically interested in.

Please go to the next page for the "Entrepreneur Self Exam."

How Good is Your Social Entrepreneurial Idea?

Please put a "1" in the box that most clearly represents the closest answer. A strong "yes" answer should be a "1" in the "A Lot" box and a strong "no" should be a "1" in the "None" box.

	None	A Little	Quite A Bit	A Lot
PERSONAL EXPERIENCE				
1. Do you have practical experience in the field of your new venture?				
2. Have you had a paying job in the broader industry where you want to launch your idea?				
3. Have you ever raised more than $50,000 for a venture of your own or for a non-profit?				
4. Have you ever launched or started a venture on your own?				
5. What level of volunteering have you done in the area of your cause?				
6. Have you ever created and implemented a new vision for something else in your life before this idea?				
7. If we asked 5 people who you interact with on a daily basis, what degree of trustworthiness would they say that you exhibit?				
RESULTS	Score	Possible		%
PERSONAL EXPERIENCE	0.0	84.8		0%

How Good is Your Social Entrepreneurial Idea?

	None	A Little	Quite A Bit	A Lot
IDEA				
8. Does your venture idea match your internal passion?				
9. Does your venture help to solve a social or environmental problem or does this idea better meet a human need than it has been met before?				
10. Can you measure the amount that it helps solve a social or environmental problem? Make sure that you have a vision for how it can be practically measured.				
11. Does your idea bring about social change by transforming traditional practice?				
12. Does your idea contain a unique and practical innovation through either an innovative product or service, the development of a different approach or a different application of known technologies?				
13. Does your unique innovation offer a competitive value proposition to the existing offerings on the market?				
14. Can the idea be scaled up or is it by definition limited to you?				
15. What is the amount of research that you have done on the internet thus far?				
16. Is your idea sustainable?				
17. Does your idea have "stickiness", ie when people experience it will they want to try it again?				
18. Survey several family members. Do they think it's a winning venture?				
19. Survey an independent business person that you respect. Do they think it's a winning venture?				
20. Survey an independent person associated with the nature of the cause. Do they think it's a winning venture?				
21. Is this potential market size and related growth significant?				
RESULTS	Score	Possible		%
IDEA	0.0	169.7		0%

How Good is Your Social Entrepreneurial Idea?

	None	A Little	Quite A Bit	A Lot
FINANCES				
22. Can you assess the cost to launch this venture?				
23. What level of confidence do you have that you will be able to obtain the funding to launch until it is profitable or if it's a non-profit, the ongoing amount needed from fund raising?				
24. **NON-PROFIT:** If you plan to set the entity up as a non-profit entity, can you reasonably see that you will achieve some degree of financial self-sustainability through fees or revenues or that you will be engaged in creating mutually beneficial partnerships with business and/or the public sector? In any case, there is a clear difference from traditional charity and a move towards community-based empowerment and sustainability. **FOR-PROFIT:** If you plan to set the entity up as a for-profit entity, does the orientation toward social and environmental value creation predominate, with financial return treated as a secondary means to an end, rather than an end in itself?				
25. Do you have at least $10,000 that you can commit to your idea?				
26. Have you put together a financial plan that includes a 3- year income statement and cash requirements?				
RESULTS	Score	Possible		%
FINANCES	0.0	60.6		0%

How Good is Your Social Entrepreneurial Idea?

	None	A Little	Quite A Bit	A Lot
OUTSIDE SUPPORT				
27. What is the level of connections that you have within the industry niche that you are seeking to enter? Can you access key constituents in the industry?				
28. Do you have 2 or more people who believe in your passion and are willing to volunteer their time to support your efforts?				
29. Do you have someone who is willing to mentor you?				
30. Do you, or someone you know, have the financial and accounting skills to help start your business?				
31. Are you and your significant other (if you have one) willing to handle the financial consequences should the venture not be successful?				
32. If you have a significant other or key family member, do they support you in this venture?				
33. Do you have any key relationships with key vendors/distributors/or people involved with helping you get your product to market?				

RESULTS	Score	Possible	%
TOTAL OUTSIDE SUPPORT	0.0	84.8	0%
TOTAL FINANCES	0.0	60.6	0%
TOTAL IDEA	0.0	169.7	0%
TOTAL PERSONAL EXPERIENCE	0.0	84.8	0%
ENTREPRENEURIAL TOTALS	**0.0**	**400.0**	**0%**

12379264R00128

Made in the USA
Lexington, KY
10 December 2011